Living in God's Kingdom on Earth

A Practical Look at Dual Citizenship

By

Charles R. Thomas

Living in God's Kingdom on Earth
A Practical Look at Dual Citizenship
by Charles R. Thomas

Printed in the United States of America

ISBN 978-1-60266-992-5

www.xulonpress.com

Reference Sources Used:

Strong, James. Abingdon's Strong's Exhaustive Concordance of the Bible with "A Key-Word Comparison of Selected Words and Phrases in the King James Version with Five Leading Contemporary Translations." Nashville: Abingdon Press, 1980.

Unger, Merrill Frederick. Unger's Bible Dictionary. Chicago: Moody Press, 1957, 1961, 1966. 38 Printing/RR/Year 87 86 85.

Dedication

I dedicate this book to those whose Godly ministry and example before me have made huge contributions to my life. I would not be the better man I am today without their deposits of spiritual values, teachings, and personal ministry. I am forever indebted to these men and women of the Kingdom.

Lee Thomas, my precious wife and life partner

Rev. Wayne and Betty Fritts

Rev. John and Nancy Kempf

Rev. Kenneth E. Hagin (deceased)

Table of Contents

Foreword

G od inspired me to write this book about living as a committed Christian, a member of God's Kingdom, in today's world. This is not an easy subject, but since God never changes, the age and culture we live in is irrelevant, except for the time line of prophetic Scripture. (That time clock is still ticking, and it has a finite ending.) Throughout man's history, there has been a consistent challenge for believers in continuing to live as native sons of their countries, yet with new responsibilities and vision for the future as born-again Christians who are part of an unseen, universal Kingdom. I would like to explore several dimensions of this dichotomy and challenge mature believers to be active lay ministers.

How do we get into this situation of being citizens of two different governments, one seen and the other unseen? Let's begin by reviewing the progression from birth till new birth and see how well we adjust to the obligations of both worlds. As humans, we are born into this world as *spirit* beings, clothed in *flesh* (body) with a *soul,* and then we go about the business of survival until death stops the short cycle of mortal life, which is but a vapor. (James 4:14 in the *Jewish New Testament* states "all you are is a mist that appears for a little while and then disappears.")

Along this linear time line of human mortality, there are those people who confess their sinful natures, accept Jesus as the Son of God, and become born again of the Spirit of God by the sacrificial blood of Jesus. They also obey Christ's commandment and are born of water through immersion baptism, fulfilling the initial Christian experience (John 3:5). They become citizens of the Kingdom of God, yet are still living on Earth. Hopefully, they now begin to make Jesus Lord of all aspects of their human lives. However, those born-again Christians keep the *same* mortal bodies (flesh) and souls (intellect, will, and emotions) while experiencing a supernatural transformation of their spirits from corruption to incorruption.

Second Corinthians 5:17, 21 declares, "If any man be in Christ, he is a new creature: old things are passed away; behold, all things are become new.... that we might be made the righteousness of God in Him." The old human spirit stained with the original Adamic sin of humanity is re-created by God in purity. There are no sin stains present in the new spirit, not even a smudge. There is no sin corruption, and the newly born spirit is transformed out of darkness and into light, with all chains of sin bondage broken.

In Acts 26:18 Jesus said these words to Saul as he was believing on Christ and being told his mission to the unregenerate of the world: "to open their eyes, and to turn them *from darkness to light,* and from the power of Satan unto God, that they may receive forgiveness of sins, and inheritance among them which are sanctified by faith that is in me" (emphasis added). First Peter 2:9 says, "But ye are a chosen generation, a royal priesthood, an holy nation, a peculiar people; that ye should shew forth the praises of him who hath called you *out of darkness into his marvelous light"* (emphasis added). Christians are new creatures in Christ Jesus! The same body and same soul exist as before, only with a new inner *spirit* of purity. Believers have become citizens of God's Kingdom on Earth, His collective Body of believers, by being children of God, with full rights and privileges. Those believers now hold two passports: one for each citizenship they possess. With those rights and privileges, though, come responsibilities. We will be examining several key areas of the responsibilities and privileges of Kingdom life throughout the chapters of this book.

Colossians 1:13–14 in the New Living Translation says, "For he has rescued us *from the kingdom of darkness* and transferred us into the Kingdom of his dear Son, who purchased our freedom and forgave our sins" (emphasis added). From this life-changing Christian experience of salvation, there are now two parallel realms, or dimensions, that new Christians confront: one in which they continue to live out their human lives as citizens of humanity — getting an education, raising a family, earning a living — and the other in which new Christians seek to obey and to please God who exists in a purely spiritual dimension and who has prepared an eternal existence for His spiritually alive people. Some folks do a better job of living simultaneously in these two different dimensions than others do, and they will be rewarded accordingly.

There are no boundaries on the capacity of God or of either of His Kingdom locations (in Heaven or on Earth). I hope to bring out some principles of living life as a citizen on Earth that may help to make that challenge less daunting to the Christian seeking fulfillment in the Kingdom of God. Our ultimate example for reference is Jesus, who simultaneously existed 100 percent as a fellow human being without Adam's sin nature and 100 percent as the Son of God. Those two different worlds coexisted in complete harmony in Him, and that is our own ultimate goal while maturing beyond our initial spiritual transformation. The key is to *strengthen the spirit* so it is consistently dominant in its influence over the body and soul as we live out our short, vaporous lives until Jesus returns in majestic power.

How does the new Christian begin to live daily in love, light, and true spirit-life in Jesus Christ while still existing in a mortal body among the spiritually dead? That is the central question around which I hope to provide some insights and recommendations in this book. How and where does a new baby Christian find spiritual food on which to grow and mature in spiritual awareness? How do I please my Heavenly Father in this life? Should I be in some kind of ministry because I am a Christian who sincerely loves God? Where do my job and family fit into my priorities? What do people mean by being "Spirit-led"?

I will offer commentary about these kinds of issues and suggest some positive steps, some dos and don'ts, and a few cautions from a Biblical perspective. My goal is to bring out some things that you may not have thought about or known how to walk out in everyday life. I will also point out some hard truths, but they should be judged in light of the Word of Truth and applied to your life as God directs you. Think outside the traditional religious box as you read through the following chapters! Please read every word of every Scripture reference given so the Bible verses can affect your thinking and challenge your ongoing spiritual development as you read through this book.

Bible Study: Results to Be Gained

Why would Psalm 119:105 in the New Living Translation tell us, "Your word is a lamp to guide my feet and a light for my path" if there was not a clear need for God's Word to provide direction along life's path? The Word, Jesus Himself, transformed by His own creation's hands into *living text* on parchment, leather, or paper, under the personal direction of God, is the One who lights your path. His light gives understanding and direction needed for getting onto the straight and narrow path and staying on it till your race is finished.

His light also lays bare the traps and snares of our enemies, both human and spirit, exposes those deeds done in darkness, and makes a source of light available to those bound in the darkness who want to be set free. This Word of life reveals the subtleties and stealth behind the assignments of evil spirits and also exposes to believers their authority over these spirits through the name of Jesus. It is the judge of truth, of prophecies, and of human motives. In John 17:17, we read of Jesus' prayer to the Father in which we learn that we are sanctified through His Word: "Sanctify them through thy truth: thy word is truth."

Beginning to establish a pattern of regular Bible study is critical for Christians, especially new Christians in the faith. "Study to show thyself approved unto God, a workman that needeth not to be ashamed, rightly dividing the word of truth.... All scripture is given by inspiration of God, and is profitable for doctrine, for reproof, for correction, for instruction in righteousness: that the man of God may be perfect, thoroughly furnished unto all good works" (2 Tim. 2:15; 3:16–17). Paul tells Timothy that these are the resulting benefits of spending time in the Word of Truth.

These truths apply to everyone, both the young (new Christian) and the old in the Lord. For new babes in Christ, though, the Word will help to get them established in the principles and boundaries of the faith. New Christians should be sponges for Bible knowledge, since they are new creatures in their spirit-beings. It no longer matters whether a man is circumcised in his flesh as long as his heart (spirit) has been circumcised. Galatians 6:15 tells us this very succinctly: "For in Christ Jesus neither circumcision availeth any thing, nor uncircumcision, but a new creature." This new birth with a new creature emerging forth is the beginning of the Christian walk in God's Kingdom.

This new creature must be fed and strengthened to be of service and to be protected from its enemies. First Peter 2:2–3 speaks to this need: "As newborn babes, desire the sincere milk of the word, that ye may grow thereby: If so be ye have tasted that the Lord is gracious." There is a good reason to feed on the milk of the Word and get strong quickly, like a baby antelope born on the African plains. The perpetual drama of life and death between predator and prey continues to play out, regardless of any one individual. As in the animal kingdom, this drama of life and death plays out with the spirit of man, except that death is eternal separation from God in torment. Believers who have newly created human spirits that are without spot or blemish soon find that there is adversity between their spirits (now in tune with God) and their still unregenerate souls and bodies. First Peter 2:11 was written to believers by a disciple who knew well this fight that ensues shortly after salvation of the spirit: "Beloved, I urge you as aliens and strangers to abstain from fleshly lusts, which wage war against the soul" (NASB).

The apostle Paul addressed the urgent need to get our fleshly bodies and carnal minds cleaned up, or perfected, in his letter to the church in Rome, found in Romans 12:1–2: "I beseech you therefore, brethren, by the mercies of God, that ye present your *bodies* a living sacrifice, holy, acceptable unto God, which is your reasonable service. And be not conformed to this world: but be ye transformed by the renewing of your *mind,* that ye may prove what is that good and acceptable, and perfect, will of God" (emphasis added). As born-again believers, if we can get our souls (minds) and bodies changed into the image of Christ Jesus, conformed to His will and submitted to the authority of our re-created spirits, we will be properly aligned with God's Kingdom on Earth *and* in Heaven, just as Jesus taught His disciples to pray (Matt. 6:9–13).

The most direct channel for getting the soul sanctified, or perfected, is through the Word of Life; it transforms the mind, and you begin to submit your will to God's plan for your life. In Second Corinthians 10:5, we are told to cast down imaginations and bring into captivity every thought to the obedience of Christ. This is achieved through immersion in the Word of Life and active spiritual warfare against thoughts implanted by evil spirits in our minds, the primary battleground.

When Paul wrote to the church at Ephesus, he gave them a key admonition about renewing their minds and recognizing their need to submit their soulish areas to the new spirit-man created in purity of spirit: "And be renewed in the spirit of your mind; And that ye put on the new man, which after God is created in righteousness and true holiness" (Eph. 4:23–24). James said it beautifully in his general letter to the Jews abroad, telling them how they could get their souls "saved" (sanctified, perfected) so the soul and spirit *together* could rule over their flesh and have dominion over carnal desires: "Receive with meekness the engrafted word, which is able to save your souls" (James 1:21).

Our flesh has not been redeemed and cannot be trusted to rule our lives. It will do anything we allow it to do. Our soul (mind, will, and emotions) directs our flesh, so we must get it transformed or renewed by the Word of God to be in line with Kingdom principles. This requires dying to self in our prayer closets and keeping the flesh "under." Paul said to the church at Corinth: "Always bearing about in the body the dying of the Lord Jesus, that the life also of Jesus might be made manifest in our body. For we which live are always delivered unto death for Jesus' sake, that the life also of Jesus might be made manifest in our mortal flesh. So then death worketh in us, but life in you" (2 Cor. 4: 10–12). Then our souls can agree with the leading of our righteous spirits, and the two together have dominion over the flesh. Only by submitting the soul to the Word of Truth and Light can it become sanctified and make right (godly) decisions of the will and the mind.

The soul can begin to resist evil thoughts injected into its thinking by evil spirits and cast down unholy imaginations. Satan's primary tactic is to approach the mind with thoughts and the flesh (body) with impure desires, since they were not regenerated—the soul is the deciding influence standing between the spirit and the flesh. Whether your soul's will sides with your flesh or your spirit in a matter depends on how strongly you stand on the Word and resist the devil. The spirit and soul of a person are so closely intertwined that only the Word of God can separate the two! Hebrews 4:12 say, "For the word of God is alive and powerful. It is sharper than the sharpest two-edged sword, *cutting between soul and spirit*, between joint and marrow. It exposes our innermost thoughts and desires" (NLT, emphasis added).

The spirit and soul make an ideal alliance of agreement against the fleshly desires and evil temptations when the soul is changed by prolonged exposure to the Word. This unity of spirit and soul in a believer can bring great change to the flesh—people do stop drinking, cursing, smoking, watching pornography, masturbating, engaging in sexual activity outside of marriage, overeating, lying, doing drugs, molesting children, stealing, and participating in other harmful, illegal, or demon-driven obsessions and compulsions. The desires of the flesh can be subdued and conquered through getting the Word-renewed soul working in cooperation with the spirit!

Ephesians 2:2–3 says, "Wherein in time past ye walked according to the course of this world, according to the prince of the power of the air, the spirit that now worketh in the children of disobedience: Among whom also we all had our conversation in times past in the lusts of our flesh, *fulfilling the desires of our flesh and of the mind;* and were by nature the children of wrath, even as others" (emphasis added). This was our unregenerate state: doomed to eternal spiritual death by our Adamic sin natures, slaves to Satan and fulfilling the carnal desires (lusts) of our bodies as directed by our minds (soul).

All praise to Jesus for setting us free from this bondage to sin and releasing us from Satan's control! He gave our spirits new birth and provided the means by which we can *choose* to get our minds renewed in Him and in His Word of Life and Truth, the Bible.

We are instructed well about life in the Spirit by Paul in his great letter to the believers in Rome in Romans 8:5–14.

> Those who are dominated by the sinful nature think about sinful things, but those who are controlled by the Holy Spirit think about things that please the Spirit. So letting your sinful nature control your mind leads to death. But letting your Spirit control your mind leads to life and peace. For the sinful nature is always hostile to God. It never did obey God's laws, and it never will. That's why those who are still under the control of their sinful nature can never please God. But you are not controlled by your sinful nature. You are controlled by the Spirit if you have the Spirit of God living in you. (And remember that those who do not have the Spirit of Christ living in them do not belong to Him at all.) And Christ lives within you, so even though your body will die because of sin, the Spirit gives you life because you have been made right with God. The Spirit of God, who raised Jesus from the dead, lives in you. And just as God raised Christ Jesus from the dead, he will give life to your mortal bodies by this same Spirit living within you. Therefore, dear brothers and sisters, you have no obligation to do what your sinful nature urges you to do. For if you live by its dictates, you will die. But if through the power of the Spirit you put to death the deeds of your sinful nature, you will live. For all who are led by the Spirit of God are children of God. (NLT)

Renewal of the soul takes place by reading the Word, hearing the Word, practicing the Word, speaking the Word, and even memorizing the Word. The Hebrews 4:12 reference stated that the Word is alive and powerful, able to effect great change. We must *see ourselves* according to God's Word and live its principles to be more than conquerors over evil. It helps to recognize that *God sees us* as the righteousness of Christ. He considers us to be more than conquerors—over poverty, fear, sickness and disease, infirmities, violence, and all other evils that we are confronted with in this Earthly life.

We must continually discipline our bodies and keep them under, or subjugated, to our spirit-soul joint dominion. Here is what Paul said of himself in 1 Corinthians 9:27: "But I buffet my body and make it my slave, lest possibly, after I have preached to others, I myself should be disqualified" (NASB). If Paul practiced self-denial and discipline in his flesh, then today's ministers and all believers should be examining themselves and denying their fleshly, or carnal, desires any expression!

Observe what Paul said to the Colossians: "If ye then be risen with Christ, seek those things which are above, where Christ sitteth on the right hand of God. Set your affection on things above, not on things on the earth. For ye are dead, and your life is hid with Christ in God" (Col. 3: 1–3). We must get our eyes focused on Jesus and spiritual life and not upon material things and lusts of the flesh. Our daily death to self in our prayer closets will allow the life of Jesus to properly establish our value system.

Jesus alone embodies truth; He is the living Word (John 1:1–5, 14), and we have Him with us continually in Scripture to illuminate our understanding of the full spiritual life available to us in Him. (I'll be discussing walking in the Spirit daily in a later chapter.) Reading the Bible renews our minds, energizes our spirits, strengthens faith, and allows us to hear the still small voice of the Holy Spirit dwelling within our human spirits. (The Holy Spirit could not dwell within us until our spirits were transformed into clean vessels for Him to reside in.) This brings about greater maturity in our fellowship with others, and most importantly, ongoing Bible study puts us in vibrant communication with our Father God. We learn how to pray and what to pray about. We begin to hear His voice more clearly and more frequently, allowing us to be more obedient to His instruction and more yielded as vessels for His use in everyday life.

First Peter 1:13–19 in the New American Standard reads as follows (emphasis added):

Therefore, *gird your minds* for action, keep sober in spirit, and fix your hope completely on the grace to be brought to you at the revelation of Jesus Christ. As obedient children, do not be conformed to the former lusts which were yours in your ignorance, but like the Holy One who called you, be holy yourselves also in all your behavior; because it is written, "You shall be holy for I am holy." And if you address as Father *the One who impartially judges according to each man's work,* conduct yourselves in fear during the time of your stay upon earth: knowing that you were not redeemed with perishable things like silver or gold from your futile way of life inherited from your forefathers, but with precious blood, as of a lamb unblemished and spotless, the blood of Christ.

With these admonitions in mind, we cannot build our foundation on our education, human reason, or the technologies of man; nor can we tolerate carnal thoughts that evolve into imaginations, best intentions, and impure motivations. Neither can we allow historical traditions of churches and religious cultures to distort or dilute the effectiveness of God's Word in our lives.

Paul pointed out in his letter to Titus that believers had to be solid in the true faith, not paying any further attention to myths and traditions of man. Titus 1:13–14 says, "This witness is true. Wherefore rebuke them sharply, that they may be sound in the faith; Not giving heed to Jewish fables, and commandments of men, that turn from the truth." These things will crowd out the Word of Truth and not allow us to gain direction for our lives and allow the Word to transform our minds. Many people who attend church, go to Mass, or participate in religious festivals do so because their family expects it or it is an integral part of their religious culture, whether Bible-based or not. The truth of God's Word will break you free of the traditions and doctrines of man.

Paul tells the church at Ephesus that Jesus washes, or cleanses, His living Church Body through His Holy Spirit with the Word of Truth and Life: "Husbands, love your wives, even as Christ also loved the church, and gave himself for it; That he might sanctify and cleanse it with the washing of water by the word" (Eph. 5:25–26). A believer who does not begin to live in and on the Word of Truth and Life will not be successful in submitting his members (body and soul) to the leadership of his re-born righteous spirit.

Jesus told His Jewish believers very clearly how important His words of life would be to them in John 8:31–32: "Then said Jesus to those Jews which believed on him, If ye continue in my word, then are ye my disciples indeed; And ye shall know the truth, and the truth shall make you free." Hear what Jesus said.

- You must get into His Word and continue in it.
- Feeding on His truths makes you His disciple indeed.
- You will eat this Bread of Life and it will reveal absolute truth to you from God. You will learn truth and it will change you, transforming and sanctifying your soulish man (mind, emotions, will). You *know* it because it becomes a part of your being!
- This accumulated truth breaks you free of all constraints, both physical and spiritual, in your soul and flesh. (Remember, your spirit has already been made the righteousness of Christ and is not bound or in need of purification as are your other members.) If you choose, you can walk victoriously through life by living and acting on the revealed truth of God.

Scripture reading will cause you to begin to hunger and thirst for more of God as you learn about His eternal character and attitudes in the Old Testament. Joshua 1:8 provides us with the correct attitude to assume concerning God's Word: "This book of the law shall not depart out of thy mouth; but thou shalt meditate therein day and night, that thou mayest observe to *do according to all that is written therein*: for then thou shalt make thy way prosperous, and then thou shalt have good success" (emphasis added). That sounds like a recipe for success in life to me!

God's character never changes. (I will bring up this critical truth later.) He is the same today as He was when talking to Joshua, as we just read, or to Moses from the burning bush on the mountain. There were many things that pleased God and many that displeased Him or that He abhorred and called abominations. Some things (acts, or works, of evil) He hated so much that He required death to the one in violation of His laws.

Fortunately for us, He allowed His Son to provide better and direct access to God than through obedience to the detailed requirements of the Mosaic Law, with its ordinances, statutes, and severe penalties. Jesus comes to us in the power of His love. His Word of Truth reveals Him to us in human characteristics that we can relate to. You will want to experience Him walking and talking with you daily as He did initially with Adam in Eden. You will start seeing and understanding the many instances throughout the Old Testament where God consistently pointed prophetically to Jesus through the strict standards of animal sacrifice, multiple and meticulous priestly rites of sacrifice, the many types of offerings required, circumcision required, temple instruments and furniture design, temple design, deliverance from Egyptian bondage, and many other examples of foreshadowing the coming Messiah.

Joseph's life and good works foreshadowed and helped bring about the Messiah to mankind. Moses was a very important type of messiah, shepherd, intercessor, prophet, and high priest that God used to foreshadow to His Jewish people the future Lamb of God who would claim those titles and more. There were many different ways in which God communicated with man, both directly and indirectly. We will look at many of these channels of communication in another, later chapter.

The Old Testament writings show us our Creator and His love for His creation. However, He benevolently gave man his own free will to exercise, as He did the angels in Heaven, and we get to see many examples of His love demonstrated for His chosen Jewish people when they were obedient, and many examples of His harsh judgment when they were disobedient. As reflected in the Ten Commandments issued to Moses, we see that the early times were a dispensation of God's imposed law and humanity's choice of response to it.

Jews exclusively were God's chosen people and they alone stood under an eternal covenant with God, with all its contemporary benefits and future promises contingent upon their living under the strict requirements of the law. The people were compelled to obey the law and required to offer sacrifices for their sins, which pointed them to the eventual sacrificial Lamb of God.

By contrast, the New Testament Scriptures reveal to us a totally new age brought about by God's Son, Jesus—one of mercy, the Messiah, redemption, atonement by Jesus' own sacrificial blood, grace, authority of the believer, existence and types of demonic activity, the priesthood of believers, baptism in water, the baptism of the Holy Spirit, gifts of the Spirit operating in believers, fruit born of the regenerated human spirit, Gentiles being grafted into the true vine, and many more tremendous examples of the fulfillment of the Mosaic Law in Jesus.

God's character has never changed from the days of the Old Testament Scriptures; He just provided a better way for man to reach Him—through His Son—and have eternal relationship. All mankind became eligible through Jesus' own blood sacrifice to have a personal relationship with God. Reading the Bible and feeding on the Bread of Life gives you wisdom, knowledge, and understanding of the spiritual state (and its privileges and authority) that you must begin to walk in as a child of God.

Through Bible study man discovers that he is given a measure of faith. The latter part of Romans 12:3 tells us that "God hath dealt to every man the measure of faith." That small amount of faith is placed by God in all people for one purpose: to allow them to call upon Jesus when they finally surrender their lives to Him, confess their sinful nature, and ask for forgiveness. Ephesians 2:8 tells us that this saving faith given to every man is a gift from God that we do nothing to gain—it is there at birth: "For by grace are ye saved through faith; and that not of yourselves: it is the gift of God."

Without that measure of faith, a sinner would not be able to communicate with God through His Son Jesus to be born again. It is analogous to the umbilical cord in a fetus. The fetus has no means of communicating directly with its mother except through that cord. Without it, death occurs. This is the identical situation for unbelievers; without using their only connection to God, they die a spiritual death. Once regenerated through the new birth, faith begins to grow and be strengthened in the new creature.

How do you increase in faith as a new Christian? Romans 10:17 teaches us a valuable lesson on where to go: "So then faith cometh by hearing, and hearing by the word of God." Feeding on the living Word of God nurtures the new spirit, strengthens it for spiritual warfare (your shield), and enables it to move into deeper relationship with God. Faith is the key that unlocks all the doors to the new believer; it is the means of accessing the things of the spirit realm and bringing them into the temporal world!

Think on these three verses from Paul's writings to the church at Corinth.

> We having the same spirit of faith, according as it is written, I believed, and therefore have I spoken; we also believe, and therefore speak.
>
> 2 Corinthians 4:13

> While we look not at the things which are seen, but at the things which are not seen: for the things which are seen are temporal; but the things which are not seen are eternal.
>
> 2 Corinthians 4:18

> For we walk by faith, not by sight.
>
> 2 Corinthians 4:7

It is the Bible that teaches man what faith consists of; otherwise, we would be wandering around in the spirit realm like a blind person unable to find anything to hold on to. Hebrews 11:1 defines faith for the believer: "Now faith is the substance of things hoped for, the evidence of things not seen." The New International translation of that key verse may provide some additional enlightenment: "Now faith is being sure of what we hope for and certain of what we do not see."

It is impossible for unbelievers to grasp that concept, since they have no spiritual understanding. Knowing what the Word of Truth (Jesus) says informs us about the things in the spirit realm that we need or have available to us. If we believe those truths, then we know for sure that they are there, and our faith (when vocalized) reaches out to access them, bringing them into existence in the physical world. They do not realize that the spirit world is *more real* than the physical, temporal world in which we live.

Faith is the means by which the believer stands on God's Word and appropriates from the spirit realm that thing or truth needed in the physical realm. You *learn* of a spiritual truth *through feeding on the Word;* you then *confess that truth* with your mouth, *which accesses* that truth in Heavenly realms and then *makes it available* to you in the physical realm. By your faith in God and His Word making it available, you now must *learn to accept* that thing and take hold of it—healing, deliverance, inspiration, interpretations of dreams and tongues, revelation, visions, spiritual gifts, blessing, favor, resources, and all manner of God-supplied treasures for His children. Those things will become reality to people who act on their faith.

Faith is required to accept the Word of Truth and profit from it. Hebrews 4:2 is Paul's powerful insight to the believing Jews about truly receiving the truth: "For unto us was the gospel preached, as well as unto them: but the word preached did not profit them, not being mixed with faith in them that heard it." We have to exercise faith when we hear or read the Word in order for it to change us. Faith is also required to receive the baptism of the Holy Ghost, stand in a ministry office within the Body of Christ, operate in the gifts of the Spirit, perform miracles and signs and wonders (as directed by the Holy Spirit) before unbelievers following the preaching of God's Word, enter into intercessory prayer, minister healing and deliverance to the oppressed, and perform many other important spiritual functions.

We know from the previous Scriptures what faith consists of and how it comes to us. One part of teaching on faith that is often omitted is *how faith operates.* Knowing and practicing this is the key part that actuates our faith and produces results. Galatians 5:6 states, "... but faith which worketh *by love*" (emphasis added). It is love that allows faith to operate in us! For some that may be a new revelation, but feeding upon the Word of Truth shows us that love is the holy oil that lubricates all our spiritual machinery. God operates toward man in a love relationship; man responds to his God out of love.

We call love a human emotion, and yet it is born of God and is part of God in us. First John 4:8, 16 says, "He that loveth not knoweth not God; for God is love.... And we have known and believed the love that God hath to us. God is love; and he that dwelleth in love dwelleth in God, and God in him." This means that God placed a measure of faith *and* love, Himself (to operate that faith), in every human being on Earth. It is His desire that all men should come to know Him and His Son in a loving relationship, and He enables every person with the means to reach out to Him. It is our choice (of will) whether or not to respond to His love and worship Him, but we have been provided the capability to do that at any time.

Once we accept His love and repent of our sinful nature, we make Jesus Lord of our lives, and God's love is perfected in us as we love our fellow man. First John 4:11–12 says, "Beloved, if God so loved us, we ought also to love one another. No man hath seen God at any time. If we love one another, God dwelleth in us, and his love is perfected in us."

I think the lack of genuine love for their fellow man is what prevents many believers from walking and praying in faith. You must feel compassion and empathy for someone you are praying for, or else your faith is impotent. If there is a "love void" in your personal walk, you will be hindered and unfulfilled in both ministering to others and attaining the call of God in your own life. Is lack of God's love in operation with faith the key reason that there is no more fruit of ministry and fruit of faith evident in today's Church?

There is one more major principle of faith that feeding on the Word of Truth should illuminate to each believer: faith must become actionable through works, or it is useless. Read James 2:14–26 for a detailed account of the value and limitations of faith relative to works. (There is a chapter devoted solely to works later in this book.) Remember, a person of actionable faith is a mighty force upon the Earth because he or she is *doing* things for God, both in the spirit realm and through good works on Earth. The end result of those good works is that God receives glory and honor.

Build up your most holy faith by feeding on God's Word of Life on a consistent basis. We cannot expect to be physically fit by exercising one week out of the year. To see positive results, we must continue for several months, and *for lasting results,* we must make exercise a part of our daily lifestyle! The same principle applies to Bible study and its effects on the individual's daily walk with God. How spiritually fit are you at this time?

Studying the Word is like making a deposit into an account at the bank; the more deposits you make, the bigger the account grows until one day you need to draw on that account for some need. The Word is always there in your human spirit, written upon your heart and ready for effective use. So invest your time in prayer and Bible study to build up your inner spirit; increase your faith; and show yourself approved unto God, able to rightly divide His Word, prepared for spiritual warfare, and equipped to help those in need.

A direct admonition for all believers is found in 2 Timothy 2:15, which we looked at earlier in this chapter: "*Study to show thyself approved* unto God, a workman that needeth not to be ashamed, rightly dividing the word of truth" (emphasis added). A maturing believer will find through Bible study that he is given all the tools he needs for spiritual strength while living productively as a citizen of Earth.

Look at Matthew 7:24–25 for a compelling reason *to feed upon* the living Word of God, which is Jesus Christ, and *to act on* His Word of Truth: "Therefore whosoever *heareth* these sayings of mine, and *doeth* them, I will liken him unto a wise man, which built his house upon a rock: And the rain descended, and the floods came, and the winds blew, and beat upon that house; and it fell not: for it was founded upon a rock" (emphasis added). You are anchoring yourself to the Rock of Ages against the storms of this physical life by studying the Word. Go beyond mere reading of the Word; memorize key Scriptures, quote the living Word out loud (as opposed to some mechanical, traditional recitation of prayers), and think on Scriptures throughout the day, as King David described.

Remember how Jesus responded to each of Satan's temptations in the wilderness: He quoted the Word of God to him in an absolute rebuke. His knowledge of the Word, in tandem with the spiritual strength gained through His fasting and prayer, allowed Him to resist every entreaty of His enemy. Are you familiar enough with the Word to repeat what God has said is absolute truth?

Let's look at one more scriptural reference in which Jesus, through a parable, asks us to evaluate how we respond to His Word: Matthew 13:3–9. Focus on the beginning and the end of these verses. Verse 3 says, "Behold, a sower went forth *to sow*"; verses 8–9 say, "But other [seed] fell into good ground, and *brought forth fruit,* some an hundredfold, some sixtyfold, some thirtyfold. Who hath ears to hear, let him hear" (emphasis added).

By that last statement, Jesus made the emphatic point that this message in a parable was critically important and that we should pay close attention to what it says. The more you submit your life to God, the more His Word takes root in good ground, is watered by the Holy Spirit, germinates in your life, and bears fruit. The fruit borne is both works of Christian labor and the fruit of a mature spirit displayed consistently: love, joy, peace, long-suffering, gentleness, goodness, faith(fulness), meekness, and temperance (see Gal. 5:22–23).

Unfortunately, many Christians simply don't know the Word. They are not encouraged by their church or denomination to read it, let alone study it. They hear the Word in bits and sound bites through Sunday school, pastoral sermons, television ministries, DVDs, or CDs. Many modern churches display Scriptures on giant screens, and most attendees quit bringing their Bibles, finding it much easier to not carry their sword with them anymore. Over time they lose their love for daily bread from the Word. They are not feeding their spirits, and their spirits become emaciated, too weak to do spiritual battle and too uninformed to discern wolves in sheep's clothing in their midst. They tend to passively accept everything whispered in their ears as gospel, merely because they can't judge the truth through personal knowledge of the Word. Study the Word, because you will have to show yourself approved through handling life's ups and downs by Bible-based knowledge and Spirit-inspired wisdom.

By your reading through the Bible, God can open your spiritual eyes to see and your ears to hear beyond the religious blindness to portions of the Word that certain churches and denominations refuse to acknowledge or to adhere. It will open your mind to an awareness of spiritual life in Christ Jesus that goes beyond tradition and will allow you to battle religious spirits that try to deceive or blind you to the Truth in its entirety. Don't allow yourself to be a slave to some denomination's non-Biblical traditions or to be blown about by every wind of doctrine that comes along. Be anchored to the Rock! The Word becomes your basis for judging all things as true and righteous, whether it is a doctrine, an evil spirit, a false prophet, or any other entity that sets itself up as being from God, speaking for God, or being God.

A believer built strong in the Word will both understand and heed the warnings given in 2 Timothy 3 and 4 concerning certain types of men to be seen and heard in the last days.

> Having a form of godliness, but denying the power thereof; from such turn away.
>
> > 2 Timothy 3:5

> *Ever learning,* and never able to come to the knowledge of the truth.
>
> > 2 Timothy 3:7, emphasis added

> For the time will come when *they will not endure sound doctrine;* but after their own lusts shall they heap to themselves teachers, having itching ears; And they shall *turn away their ears from the truth,* and shall be turned unto fables.
>
> > 2 Timothy 4:3–4, emphasis added

Are you strong in God's Word? Do you know where the individual books are located within the Old and New Testaments? Is your Bible study regular and done in a quiet environment? Do you just read through the Bible as a book; or do you truly study it, feeding on it, gaining strength from it, and writing it upon your mind? Do you pray for God to enlighten you while reading His Word, revealing new layers of understanding in familiar Scriptures? Are you prepared to enter spiritual battle and stand on God's Word against demon spirits? Can you wield the two-edged sword of the Spirit in battle without cutting yourself?

My prayer is that you will cherish the Word of Life, value it above all books of man, and continually recognize that it is Jesus speaking and moving from the pages of holy text. John 1:1–4 speaks to the great revelation to man: "In the beginning (before all time) was the Word (Christ), and the Word was with God, and the Word was God Himself. He was present originally with God, all things are made and came into existence through Him; and without Him was not even one thing made that has come into being. In Him was Life and the Life was the Light of men" (AMP).

Discipleship

The term *discipleship* seems on the surface to be a word that has little chance of misunderstanding or confusion, but that is precisely what has happened since Jesus admonished His own disciples and us to disciple other new believers. This is a distinctly different process from when Jesus charged Peter to feed His sheep. I will talk later about pastoral care, nurturing, and teaching given to those placed under the ministry of called and chosen shepherds in the Body of Christ. Here in this chapter, we will focus on how one person has a direct, beneficial, progressive, and Christ-centered influence, in word and by example, on another person.

The accelerated rate at which the moral and ethical fiber of humanity has devolved over the past one hundred years makes the concept of discipleship of utmost importance in each body of believers today. Where will new Christians and young Christians see examples of righteous living demonstrated except from mature men and women who truly walk the walk?

God's ideal for discipleship starts in the family, with a believer at the head. The man and woman in marriage disciple their children, who learn from the earliest age to love God, to understand His character, to learn His Word of Truth, to fear His judgment, and to practice walking in the light, doing good works that bear good fruit. Let us look at two examples from many in Scripture that show how long ago this discipleship process was expected to be followed, from Adam's time in Eden onward through time.

1. Deuteronomy 6:2, 7 (emphasis added):

> That thou mightest fear the Lord thy God, to keep all his statutes and his commandments, which I command thee, *thou, and thy son, and thy son's son,* all the days of thy life; and that thy days may be prolonged.... And *thou shalt teach them diligently unto thy children,* and shalt talk of them when thou sittest in thine house, and when thou walkest by the way, and when thou liest down, and when thou risest up.

It is clear to see how the continuity is maintained in walking in God's ways by the process described here. It is not limited to just your immediate progeny but also to your grandchildren and beyond.

The children were immersed in the things of God: how to be led by Him, how He spoke to people, which consequences followed disobedient acts and words, how to stay under His blessing, and so forth. Every successive generation, even before the time when writings existed among man, was instructed by God to do this continual teaching.

The ways of God were most likely passed orally from parent to child within the family, then outward to the extended family, and then outward to those people within the parents' circle of influence in their community. The result was effective, as we can see from the lives of people descended from Adam who were diligent to disciple their children and successive generations.

2. In Psalm 78:3–6 (emphasis added), the psalmist is reminding the people of Israel of their obligations concerning God's laws. Follow the thread of responsibility within the family unit to ensure that God's intentions and instructions are clearly known by all and followed, even to later generations:

> Which we have heard and known, and *our fathers have told us.* We will *not hide them from their children, shewing to the generation to come* the praises of the Lord, and

his strength, and his wonderful works that he hath done. For he established a testimony in Jacob, and appointed a law in Israel, which *he commanded our fathers, that they should make them known to their children:* That *the generation to come* might know them, *even the children which should be born;* who should arise and *declare them to their children.*

For many believers in today's society, salvation and the Lordship of Christ came at an older age and not from within the family unit or church during childhood. These new believers typically do not already know the ways of God and need immediate instruction and guidance to get their feet planted properly in the Kingdom of God. Discipleship for them is a progressive maturation through intimate relationships with more mature Christians.

I use the word *intimate* because that relationship has to be very close, caring, trusting, and open to receive. It does not imply nor should it ever involve any sexual relationship. Men should disciple men; women should disciple women. There must exist a high level of confidence between brothers in Christ Jesus (or between sisters) so that the process of discipleship will be productive by virtue of the one being discipled having a prayerful and submissive attitude, wanting to learn how to be a person of integrity and bear spiritual fruit while going about daily life.

The one responsible for discipling his brother must bear a great sense of responsibility before God for what he instructs and teaches his brother in Christ, and *he must, above all, be a consistent example* of a godly man in his personal life. This discipling process takes time, effort, and patience, but the final product is very rewarding, similar to a loving father teaching his son how to act and talk like a man, not a boy any longer.

Jesus had to spend much quality time with His chosen disciples during the three years He had available, teaching them and showing them spiritual principles at work, demonstrating the gifts of the Spirit, answering their many questions, and preparing them for their own ministries that God had called them to. Without this discipleship process occurring through living life with and receiving instruction from Jesus, how could these men ever have become effective apostles, the highest ministry office in the Body of Christ?

As a young Christian, how do you learn to get your life together according to God's principles? Whom do you ask, and where do you go? You will not get much practical information on daily life only while listening to the pastor's sermon from the pulpit. He is busy saying what God has instructed him for that specific time, calling the unregenerate to repentance and building up the local body of believers. You will not get it in Sunday school. It will not come from the fellowship and general Bible discussion that occurs during a Bible study or home cell-group meeting.

So how do you learn how to be the priestly head of your household, to manage finances according to Biblical principles, to teach and disciple children, to fully submit your life to God, to dress appropriately, to implement Christian principles at work, to pray for the sick, to cast out demons, and so forth, when you have not been a Christian long, have a terrible marriage relationship, cannot balance a checkbook, alienate co-workers on the job, withhold tithes from your church, are self-centered, are materialistic, and indulge in hidden sin that no one else knows about? One of the ways to turn around these kinds of situations and circumstances is to submit yourself to someone whom you respect as a mature Christian, whose family is spiritually healthy, whose household is in order, who walks in integrity, whose reputation is above reproach, who loves God, and who bears the fruit of the Spirit in his life. If you don't know anyone like that, ask your pastor for a man (or woman) to disciple you! He doesn't have to be a minister, but he does have to demonstrate spiritual maturity and have a good report within the church and community to qualify as one who can impart godly wisdom to another for righteous and productive living.

Titus 2 provides a good example of this. This Scripture explains how daily righteous living among believers is to be taught and on whom the responsibility to teach it falls— the older, more mature members of the group! It instructs (not asks) the older men and women in the church to give instruction to the younger men and women. Titus 2:3–5 says: "The older women likewise, that they be reverent in behavior, not slanderers, not given to much wine, teachers of good things; that they admonish the young women to love their husbands, to love their children, to be discreet, chaste, homemakers, good, obedient to their own husbands, that the word of God may not be blasphemed."

Perhaps the younger women were unable to cook, wore provocative clothing, were rebellious toward their husbands, or gossiped about others. Titus may have seen that the younger men were boastful, arrogant, selfish, not understanding how to serve others, making rash decisions, mistreating their wives, spending foolishly, and on and on. Titus wanted the more mature believers to disciple the new believers and the less mature ones in that body of believers. This is the process of discipleship, and it is best accomplished between believers in committed relationship, when bathed in prayer and based on Biblical principles. For discipleship to work and fruit to be borne, there has to be accountability for positive change, or else it is little more than giving advice and hoping it helps.

Unfortunately, the concept of discipleship has been poorly communicated by ministers and, even more so, poorly *practiced* within the Body of Christ. At the end of typical church services, we might have an altar area filled with people, but as time passes, we see little personal growth and maturity in the Body of Christ. We need each other, and discipleship plays a valuable role in the maturation of young Christians within the Body of Christ.

Some people have been turned off by previous discipleship movements that seemed to be self-serving and required an exaggerated level of submission. Those mistakes don't negate the Lord's instruction for us to disciple nations, which takes place one person at a time. There may be unbalanced relationships or even counterfeits to arise, but God always has someone available with the real goods. Form a close relationship with the right person (one whom you can receive from), and see what God does to raise your awareness of His principles, to instill Bible-based character, and to stretch the cords of your tent to begin to bear spiritual fruit in your daily life.

Please open your Bible to Genesis 18 and 19. This might seem like an odd place in Scripture to teach on discipleship. But God provides a profound set of lessons about many aspects of discipleship in these two chapters that happen to focus on sin and its judgment for the resulting iniquity. I won't go over all the Scriptures but will highlight those points and verses that involve strong evidence of successful discipleship.

- Abraham was a righteous man. Without benefit of any written commandments from God, he had been schooled in the things of God by his forefathers, orally given from one directly to the other. He knew exactly what had happened in Eden a few generations back and may have received direct instruction from Noah on doing the will of God. Remember that lifetimes were very long back then, not as they are now. Noah lived to be 950 years old, so he outlived many generations of his progeny and was able to pass on the steps of a righteous, obedient man to hundreds, or even thousands, of his descendants before he died. (Think how many were schooled in the ways of the Lord by Methuselah before he died at 969 years of age.) When Abraham's father, Terah, died, Abraham then adopted Lot (his nephew) and raised him, instructing Lot in obedience to God's will and being the example to Lot of a godly man. Did this training take?

- When Jesus and two angels appeared to Abram (as he was still called in chapter 18), he immediately displayed the characteristics (fruit) of an obedient and yielded life although he was ultra-rich for that era. He bowed himself before them (obeisance); he showed sincere hospitality to strangers; he welcomed these aliens into his home and referred to himself as their servant; he supplied water for them to wash with and to drink (a precious commodity in the land); he prepared the best food for refreshment (even sacrificed a calf); and he kept them company while tending to all their needs. This was serving others in humility, being a good steward of the possessions God had given into his hand, and loving others as himself (as Jesus later taught us).

- When it was divulged to Abram that the visitors were going to destroy the city of Sodom because of widespread sodomy, he immediately began to intercede for those righteous people who might be killed along with the wicked. (A good time to remember that it rains on both the just and the unjust.) On what basis could Abram negotiate with the Lord over the lives of people he didn't know (except Lot's family), especially when he was told the angels intended to destroy the entire city if they found it as evil and debauched as the sounds ascending from it into Heaven seemed to indicate? It would be a serious matter to get between Jesus and two angels going to destroy a city!

But Abram was allowed to intercede, even to the point of repeated pleadings for fewer and fewer righteous ones present in order for the city to be spared destruction. It was for three reasons that I can see. First, it was acknowledged by the Lord in Genesis 18:18–19 that Abram was a righteous man, *"that he will command his children and his household after him, and they shall keep the way of the Lord"* (v. 19, emphasis added). This is discipleship as God intended—entire households and each subsequent generation of children.

Second, Abram's repeated intercessions were based upon his firsthand knowledge of God and His attitudes. He had spent time in prayer and worship before God. He had written upon his heart the things told by his forefathers and treasured them. He knew and understood his God. This allowed him to state what he knew to the holy strangers: God would not want innocent people to die unjustly.

In Genesis 18:25, Abram went further and got very personal in his bold question: "Shall not the Judge of all the earth do right?" Abram knew how to plead his case. This is precisely how Jesus dealt with Satan's temptations, reminding him boldly of God's Word of Truth. Abram declared the truth of God that he knew was absolute at that time.

Third, Abram never budged from a position of humility before the Lord in these pleadings for the lives of righteous ones in Sodom. He reminded the Lord in Genesis 18:27 that he was but dust and ashes. Abram never let desperation, fear of the Lord (standing directly in front of Him, in His way), humiliation, anger, frustration, rebellion, or pride keep him from focused intercession for those righteous ones in Sodom who were undeserving of destruction. He knew his place in the grand scheme of Earthly things but never lost sight of who he was before God: he came from dust and would return one day to dust.

Abram was able to whittle down the number of righteous required to ten before the strangers left, although they proved to be more merciful than that when in Sodom. Personally, I think God mercifully spared the eventual four lives out of love for His servant Abram, who had put his own safety at risk while blocking the way and negotiating with the Lord about limits of judgment while pleading for the lives of others.

- Chapter 19 tells of two angels remaining after Jesus left them before they entered Sodom. Personally, I don't think Jesus could stand in the midst of such evil and perversion as existed in the city, so He sent the angels of judgment to do their work. Jesus had met and communed with Abram and had witnessed how he handled himself (very humble, highly disciplined, depending on his relationship with God) when confronted with the situation, and Jesus was satisfied.

We now come to Lot, who, like Abram, was sitting at the city entrance where he could welcome strangers. Perhaps the wealthiest man in the city, he graciously rose to meet the two angels, bowed before them, and pleaded with them to come into his house and spend the night. They could wash their dirty feet, he said. They said they would spend the night in the streets, but he insisted that they accept his hospitality. He then made them a feast.

Does this man sound familiar? Certainly, for he was properly discipled by his uncle Abram. We might call him a mini-Abram because Abram had poured himself into teaching Lot the ways of God and how important it was in life to be yielded and obedient, to put others first, and to love and fear the living God. That discipleship process successfully transferred those desires, works, and integrity to the next generation.

• When his guests were in jeopardy of being abused by the men of Sodom, Lot interceded for them at great risk to himself. He had learned this God-given ministry from Abram. We then see that Lot's righteous attempt at persuading the sodomites to leave his guests alone led him to offer as a substitute his two virgin daughters still at home. (God had instructed righteous men to serve and to protect anyone, even a stranger, who was invited into their homes.)

The mob became enraged with his pleadings and stalling, and they were going to attack Lot. That stance on his doorstep in defense of his guests was not admirable, noble, nor any other human quality. The motivation came from years of godly training from Abram, watching Abram intercede for other people and eventually acting on behalf of God when others were in danger or need.

The parallels here in these two chapters between Abram and Lot exemplify beautifully the benefits of active discipleship as God intended. As humans, if we *see, hear, and do* things, we will remember them for a long time. Abram was a living example to Lot, and it stuck!

There are other examples of active discipleship shown throughout the Bible after which the one being discipled was able to carry forth the work of the Lord in a mature leadership role: Elijah and Elisha, Moses and Joshua, Jesus and His disciples, and Paul and several different men (Barnabas and Silas) who learned and traveled under his ministry.

My wife and I can both speak to the profound and positive change that occurs when a person has been discipled. We spent several valuable years under the leadership of a minister and his wife who carefully and lovingly spoke into our lives those godly principles that we needed to grow beyond the troubles and pettiness of our Christian existence at that time. They led by example; they held us accountable for what we learned from them; and they spent quality time with us each week, both one on one and together. That discipleship process forever changed us, and we are very appreciative of God for bringing us under their ministry during that time in our lives. Discipleship brings forth the following fruit when hearts and minds are yielded to learn through instruction and by example:

1. Submitting to authority; being obedient to the principles and laws (rules) of church, secular government, employers, and family structure
2. Being obedient to God, whether from His Word, His voice within your spirit, or direction from others
3. Taking responsibility for yourself and others
4. Producing works by actuating faith in everyday life
5. Learning to serve others in humility: neighbors, family, friends, and colleagues
6. Showing honor and respect to all authorities, governmental, ministerial, and familial
7. Managing finances in a responsible manner, with God's principles in operation
8. Becoming a good and faithful steward of what God has put into your hands
9. Accepting and taking your proper role within your family
10. Becoming planted in your local church, serving others through the gifts and talents that God has placed within you

Daily Priorities

This subject is not easily laid out in a pattern to strictly follow since there are numerous areas that need attention daily, some are occasional issues to deal with, and a few are absolutes. To help clarify the order of priorities, I have made a list in descending order of importance. Let's explore these and try to gain the bigger perspective on what is most relevant as a Christian seeking to please God while living as a mortal. With the proper helicopter view, most other things in life begin to fade into the background as being so much less important, and distractions become merely background noise.

Listed below is my list of daily priorities, what is most important and takes precedence over the others that follow. Think of these as concentric rings, with you and God together in the center ring. For you, that single relationship is the most important one in your life. If you have that as priority number one, your relationship with your spouse will then blossom as the result of the fruit borne from number one. As the numbered order of the list increases, so does your sphere of influence.

1. My relationship with God
2. My relationship to my spouse
3. My relationship to my family members
4. My job/work/employment responsibilities

5. My church, the immediate body of believers that I relate to and am planted within for corporate fellowship, worship, teaching, and prayer
6. All other issues of life

Some people may look at that list and disagree with the relative order of priorities, so let's explore the areas listed above. A happy, productive life with your family and church while pleasing God and maturing in Him is attainable only when realizing and adhering to priorities. Otherwise, daily decisions become situational or circumstance-based, and you begin to do things outside of a solid framework for consistent success. How much quality time do you spend in each priority area of your life?

First, God has to become the single most important person in your life, whether you remain single or get married, whether you become a minister or not. He created you, formed you in the womb, allowed His only Son to be sacrificed for your sins, drew you to repentance by His Spirit, placed His Spirit within your human spirit, leads you through the rest of your life, joined you to a mate in a holy bond (if you are married), and has prepared eternal life for you with Him in Heaven. Nothing else in this life compares to that level of utmost dependency, love, and service.

Depending on your relationship to Him, He also heals, protects, delivers from oppression, provides, and blesses you. He blesses your marriage and allows it to grow deep and steady as a rock. Your employment is blessed with success, and He gives you favor with men and women, opens doors of opportunity, sets up situations for you to shine in, and allows you to work by the sweat of your brow as all mankind is subject to do. My point is that God is at the top of the list because everything under Him is less than He is. He created it, He provided it, and your life will be successful in those areas if you place Him at number one.

What does the Word of Truth say? Look at Jesus' words in Matthew 22:36–38: "Master, which is the great commandment in the law? Jesus said unto him, Thou shalt love the Lord thy God with all thy heart, and with all thy soul, and with all thy mind. This is the first and great commandment." This reply is very clearly a defining moment for the elite Jewish lawyers in their pursuit of Jesus through His own words. He distilled all the Jewish law (both what God had given and what they had added) into that single nutshell of priority—loving God with all your body, soul, and spirit—which they themselves were in violation of.

As those words from Jesus' mouth crystallized in their minds, they had to make a choice: either repent or fall away in shame from the crowd. Jesus consistently brought people to confront change, make decisions, and obey the Father. Today's Christian has a pure, regenerated *spirit* that truly loves God. The daily battle he faces is getting the *soul and body* to love Him completely too! That commandment is our challenge today, as it was in the days that Jesus walked upon the Earth.

The *second* priority is your spouse. Look at your spouse as God-given, and give thanks daily for your spouse's companionship and love. From your spouse, you should be receiving human love that is second only to that of your parents, initially, and which will ultimately surpass that of your parents in its fullness. If God is not number one, then many marriages will fail. If He is your number one priority, He will bless your marriage, and the two of you together will be greater than the sum of both of you individually.

God provided a unique relationship for a man and woman in marriage that is not equaled by any other human relationship and which constitutes a most powerful force for ministry, whether needed in rearing children or in spiritual matters. Let's look at a few of the important aspects of marriage that the Bible presents.

1. In Genesis 2, we see that God looked upon man and knew that companionship and mutual service were needed for completeness. He formed Eve from one of Adam's ribs and blessed their union. In verse 24, Adam prophesied that the marriage union, under God's blessing, resulted in the two becoming *one flesh* in God's eyes. Incredible! That is the ultimate in achieving unity within human relationships.

   Malachi 2:15 confirms God's view on the uniqueness of the sacred marriage relationship: "Didn't the Lord make you one with your wife? In body and spirit you are his" (NLT). This intimate union is precisely the one that Jesus used consistently to typify His future return as a groom joining together with His Bride for the marriage feast. We will be joined together with Him in both our spirits and resurrected bodies!

2. The marriage relationship is consummated in sexual relationship, which is a sacred act between a man and woman joined by God. No other act brings greater intimacy in a relationship. There is something powerful and spiritual that occurs during sex between husband and wife, something that results in the joining or connection of their human spirits as well as their bodies.

Throughout the Old and New Testaments, God repeatedly issued laws (commandments) concerning illicit, unholy sexual relationships between married spouses and others, unmarried individuals, humans with animals, men with men, and various perversions of sexual behavior (Rom. 1). There was to be no misuse of the sacred, procreative organs that man was given for perpetuating his seed.

Scriptures abound where fornication and adultery were forbidden, where sodomy and whoredom were abhorred, and where death was the penalty for these serious acts under the Old Testament law. Why would God impose such severe judgment on a human act unless the human sexual union was unique among His creation, was considered sacred by the Creator, and was intended for pleasure and divine procreation solely within the sanctity of the marriage relationship? It has to be due to the existence and involvement of the human spirit, which is God-breathed into every fetus as He forms it in the womb (Job 31:15; Isa. 44:2, 24).

There are severe spiritual and physical penalties for sexual relationships outside of marriage, as seen in the heavy price being paid in today's world of pleasure-seeking: mental and emotional instability, demonic oppression, divorce, abortion, homosexuality, bestiality, child molestation, pornography, sexually transmitted diseases, cohabitation, infanticide, a global host of orphans, deformities, incest, and many other similar problems of deep spiritual darkness. People should look to God for direction about whom they should be yoked to because the acts of becoming unequally yoked have direct physical and spiritual consequences.

Second Corinthians 6:14–16, 17–18 speaks to this issue and the inherent opposing forces in conflict.

> Be ye not unequally yoked together with unbelievers: for what fellowship hath righteousness with unrighteousness? And what communion hath light with darkness? And what concord hath Christ with Belial? Or what part hath he that believeth with the infidel? And what agreement hath the temple of God with idols? For ye are the temple of the living God.... Wherefore come out from among them, and be ye separate, saith the Lord, and touch not the unclean thing; and I will receive you, and will be a Father unto you, and ye shall be my sons and daughters, saith the Lord Almighty.

Christians should never let their regenerated spirits (of light, love, and life) come into direct contact, through sexual union, with spirits still in darkness and with the bondage of sin. Although I cannot define the consequences, we know from past and present human experience that they are severe and degrading!

This may be a good point at which to offer some further comment about the human body and intimacy outside of marriage, since young people are being barraged with advertising, fashion, peer pressure, television, movies, and music that are saturated with blatant sexual imagery and enticement. Also, in the mainstream now are appeals for various means of desecrating the body: cutting, stripping skin with subsequent scarring, tattooing, dyeing, piercing of all types and in all places, implanting plastic and metal objects under the skin, and other forms of body "art" and mutilation.

First, a few words to give on illicit sexual relationships. Let's visit 1 Corinthians 6:15–20.

Know ye not that your bodies are the members of Christ? Shall I then take the members of Christ, and make them the members of an harlot? God forbid. What? Know ye not that he which is joined to an harlot is one body? For two, saith he, shall be one flesh. But he that is joined unto the Lord is one spirit. Flee fornication. Every sin that a man doeth is without the body; but he that committeth fornication sinneth against his own body. What? Know ye not that your body is the temple of the Holy Ghost which is in you, which ye have of God, and ye are not your own? For ye are bought with a price: therefore glorify God in your body, and in your spirit, which are God's.

This purity of body is a heavy responsibility for young people, and Satan wants to entrap every adolescent and single adult into promiscuous behavior in order to pervert God's perfect design and to adversely impact future marriage relationships.

First Thessalonians 4:3–5 adds to the sacredness of the body, the temple of God: "For this is the will of God, even your sanctification, that ye should abstain from fornication: That every one of you should know how to possess his vessel in sanctification and honour; Not in the lust of concupiscence, even as the Gentiles which know not God." Certainly, experiencing the stimulation of the body is pleasurable, and achieving orgasm is very intense, but Christian young people who experiment with sexual activities before marriage are degrading themselves in multiple areas. Some of these areas are discussed below.

- *Spiritual whoredom.* Your human spirit, which is one with Jesus by the presence of the Holy Spirit within your spirit, now rejects Him and joins itself to the spirit of another person, usually an unbeliever. Even if another believer is the partner, the intimacy is not sanctified, because of the lack of blessed marriage before God.

  Spiritual whoredom with idols has always been an abomination to God. In the Old Testament, God looked upon it as so extreme that He had the Hebrews put to death those who practiced such folly. Today the sexual acts and relationships become substitute idols to the individuals involved because of the effects on the spirit, which has been re-created by God and is the dwelling place for His Spirit.

- Because the sexual intimacy between partners is sinful to God, the activities can open the door to demonic spirits affecting the soul and body. The more frequent and intense the sin, the stronger the evil spirits can entrench themselves in the soul (emotions, mind, and will) and body of the participants. Then, prolonged yielding to the carnal desires inflamed by the demons allows other spirits to enter: pornography, masturbation, voyeurism, child molestation, and various other spirits of perversion.

  Spirits of depression, paranoia, suicide, and obsession are examples of the wide range of demonic entities that can have access to the mind and emotions. When a strongman has taken control, deliverance ministry is required to break that controller's power and cast out all the associated spirits. By then, and if successful, the young person involved has missed out on all that God designed for complete fulfillment within the marriage relationship.

- *Degradation of the body.* The above Scriptures are clear on the two bodies becoming one and this being a unique sin, a sin against the human body itself. How does the effect on the body manifest? One big area is sexually transmitted diseases (STDs) that may ravage the body and key organs, leading to reproductive problems (with the uterus, Fallopian tubes, testes), miscarriages, stillbirths, spontaneous abortions, cancers (of the cervix, vocal cords), mental illness, death, and other complications of infection by pathogenic microorganisms.

  Another aspect of the body's vulnerability is in various manifestations of demonic spirits that have entered into the physical body. This may be in the form of fetal deformities;

mutations; cancers; sexual perversions that harm the body (sadomasochism, anal sex); spasms; jerks or tics; compulsions; exaggerated actions, responses, and appetites; excessive thirst; and irritability. These are but just a few of the many possible manifestations of demons in human bodies.

- If both the spiritual purity is compromised and the body is surrendered to carnal pleasure, demonic strongholds can pervert the normal forms of sexual union and aberrations develop through experimentation or willful submission to the power of stronger spirits ruling others. These can be developmental by choice or congenital as a result of some spiritual power or curse affecting a parent or ancestor.

  This area covers homosexuality, bestiality, necrophilia, and many other tragic spiritual conditions of depravity in mankind that separate him (or her) from God. These particular sins were such an abomination to God in Old Testament times that He penalized participants with death so the practices would be permanently broken in each family line affected.

  However, those same spirits of depravity still roam the Earth today, and each person has to resist their influence. These aberrations seem to be rampant and more open in modern society, and we see the spiritual and social affects on society and individuals.

- Remember that in the God-ordained marriage relationship between a man and woman of faith, everything is holy and allowed in the marriage bed between the two consenting mates. Everything else in the way of sexual contact between people is sin in God's eyes. "Marriage is honourable in all, and the bed undefiled: but whoremongers and adulterers God will judge" (Heb. 13:4). "Know ye not that the unrighteous shall not inherit the Kingdom of God? Be not deceived: neither fornicators, nor idolaters, nor adulterers, nor effeminate, nor abusers of themselves with mankind, nor thieves, nor covetous, nor drunkards, nor revilers, nor extortioners, shall inherit the Kingdom of God" (1 Cor. 6:9–10).

• *Unplanned pregnancy.* This unfortunate consequence of sex outside of marriage compounds the problem of the original sin. Now major life decisions have to be made by the biological parents, if they both are known, and the long-term effects are lifelong. The couple may decide to marry, but the event will not be ideal (timing, pressures, finances, situations in education or existing families that require the involvement of others or dropping out of programs or jobs, true godly love as the basis for the relationship, and many other factors). If no marriage is planned, then how is the support of the child to be handled for many years to come? Unfortunately, the innocent child may be put up for adoption, committed to an orphanage, raised by relatives, or simply thrown into the river (infanticide), as is done in some countries.

A most tragic compounding of pregnancy problems occurs when the mother decides to abort the unborn child. This murder of the baby exacts a heavy price on the mother and anyone else involved in the decision and the act of abortion: guilt of murder, complicity of medical facilities, possible alienation of family and friends, thoughts of suicide, demonic oppression, possible infertility problems in the future, depression, various mental disorders, and many more. Abortion is an abomination to God, and many millions of unrepentant people will be judged for their actions or complicity in the decision.

Second, to apply body art is to desecrate the human body that is the temple of God. Our bodies are intended for the indwelling and worship of our God, not to be adorned and self-worshipped by man. Pagan religions and atheistic religions of history are steeped in practices of body art and body piercing. The people of these religions were idolaters who did not value the body as the repository of their gods. They sought to adorn themselves through these practices and derived much pride in their "display" of their bodies, often to attract the opposite sex. Their practices were also closely linked to sexual practices such as initiation rites, group sex, temple prostitution (both male and female), perversions, and sexual sacrifices.

Christians are to be a holy people, a peculiar people, and living stones in His blood-bought temple. I think of tattoos as graffiti on the walls of God's temple. Leviticus 19:28 says "Ye shall not make any cuttings in your flesh for the dead, nor print any marks upon you: I am the Lord." Piercings are holes in the structures of the temple, weakening it. The white stones of the holy temple in some people are marked with scratches, cuts, and ink stains that mar the appearance of their vessel before God. These practices are demon-inspired and make a mess, both physically and spiritually, of the temple of God. We need to respect our bodies and our God enough to worship Him in other prescribed ways (than physical desecration) that bring Him glory and honor.

3. God's divine plan is for progeny to be the blessed fruit of the Christian marriage union of a man and woman. Many times in the Old Testament, we read of instances where God opened the womb of a barren woman so that she might bear fruit. Psalms 127:3 reads "Lo, children are an heritage of the Lord: and the fruit of the womb is his reward."

If this divine proclamation through King David were truly believed and children were treated as such on an extensive basis throughout Christianity, the Kingdom of God on Earth would be growing by huge numbers daily, since Christian parents would be discipling their children in the ways of the Lord and leading them to salvation. There would not be nearly as many orphans, children shared by split families, millions of illegitimate babies, and abandoned children living on the streets of major cities around the world. Instead, we would see numerous miniking-doms of believers, populated by many healthy family units that cherish their children and nurture them. Those children would be reared, taught, and appreciated as blessings from God.

There are several passages in the Old and New Testaments where God called to ministry, anointed, and even filled with the Holy Spirit fetuses in the wombs of their mothers. Read the first two chapters of Luke for a thrilling description of how God can perform great works even through unborn babies of dedicated parents. Each succeeding generation of children shapes the world in its own view. As God directs them, the parents must direct the children.

4. There is no greater unity on Earth as that which exists within the Christian marriage relationship. The two members are physically and spiritually intimate, achieving a level of unity that is unsurpassed in human relationships. How can this be of benefit to the marriage and to others? Look at Matthew 18:19–20: "Again I say unto you, that if two of you shall agree on earth as touching any thing that they shall ask, it shall be done for them of my Father which is in Heaven. For where two or three are gathered in my name, there am I in the midst of them."

What greater agreement on Earth can be made than within the marriage relationship? God wants marriage partners to pray together, to leverage their unique depth of unity to achieve results in matters of prayer. I always look for dedicated couples to join in agreement with me for things that I need to cover in prayer. I welcome Christian couples to visit me and pray for my healing when I am sick or injured. Take advantage of that added power of agreement within marriage. Don't neglect to pray together: for your jobs, your children, your church body, your spiritual growth, and all important issues of life.

Here is an example of the power of united prayer of agreement in our lives. I was the youth minister at a church, and it was Wednesday evening on a summer night. Our church ran a bus into several neighborhoods to pick up children who wanted to come but had no way to get there. Standing outside the family center/gym building, I noticed a group of kids getting off the bus and heading to the building. One little girl, whom I had never seen before, was skipping and running along to class with the rest. I got her attention and stooped down to talk for a minute with this cute little six- or seven-year-old girl.

As I started to speak, I suddenly noticed that her hands looked horrible, as if she had advanced leprosy eating the flesh from her hands and fingers. It was difficult to speak to her, since I had never seen such a condition outside of medical texts. She told me that the doctor had told her mother that she (the little girl) had some form of psoriasis. I asked her if I could pray for her hands, and she said okay. I called my wife over and asked her to join in agreement with me for the healing of this girl's hands. Right there, with kids running and giggling all around us in that big patch of asphalt, we grasped her hands and prayed, in unity, the prayer of healing and deliverance from that tormenting disease. When we finished our prayer, she skipped off to class, and we went our way.

One hour later as I was leaving that building and heading over to the church sanctuary, I saw that little girl running toward the bus to be taken home to her housing project. I called to her and went over to ask if she had enjoyed the kids' service and if she would be back. Before I could open my mouth to speak, I was struck dumb for an instant when I looked at her hands and saw that they were completely healed. There were no lesions, no white splotches, no discolorations of any type! The skin was normal, with no evidence that there had ever been a vicious disease attacking the flesh.

I held her hands in mine, unable to talk. She smiled at me and ran off to the bus, probably not understanding the divine touch she had received from the Great Physician that night. I never saw that girl again but take great joy in knowing that my wife and I together were able to stand strong in agreement for her healing and that our great God honored our request.

5. Marriage is usually the first close relationship of accountability that people have on their own as adults in which they have to walk out the principles by which they intend to live their lives. Will you act and talk one way in front of your co-workers and buddies and then be different when you go home to your spouse?

Will your spouse see you reading or watching things that are contradictory to your professed walk with God? Will you show your spouse the commitment, respect, service, and sincere love that Jesus shows His Bride? Will you learn to serve and honor your spouse? If you have been properly discipled as a child growing up under your parents' Christian care and instruction, you should have little difficulty making the transition to independence while continuing in obedience to God's principles of righteous living on Earth.

The *third* priority is your family, both those who came before you and those who come after you. On various branches around and throughout that family tree are your relatives: cousins, nieces and nephews, aunts and uncles, and in-laws by marriage into your family. If you have any question about God's attitude concerning the importance of family, start reading in Genesis; you will be more than convinced of His emphasis on family obligations, rights of the firstborn, family bonds, inheritance matters, and blood relationships before He ever gets to Moses or David and the messianic lineage.

Your family ancestors determine your genetic makeup and physical appearance, but they also determine whether your present-day members are under God's blessing. When God saw the obedience and upright hearts of people throughout history, He usually blessed them and their heirs for many generations, both spiritually and materially. Think of how influential a person could be who is seen as a dedicated, Spirit-filled child of God, full of wisdom, knowledge, and understanding applied in business or government. That type of person will be in great demand; people want to be around and work under successful leaders.

The family environment is the first and most important place for discipleship to occur. Where else in our society are children going to see and learn the principles of authority, submission, obedience, serving, honoring, good works, and other characteristics of Jesus? The results are good for a lifetime!

Parents must understand that this responsibility comes from God during the rearing of children that He blesses them with. Children must come to an understanding as they mature that Mom and Dad are their protectors, their supply, and their instructors on how to prepare for life outside the home while living for God as Christians.

Children must be taught self-discipline, respect for others, how to serve others, who God is and what must be done to know Him, how to pray, how to develop good Bible-study habits, what giving involves, and all the other important issues of the Christian walk. Where will children first see and learn principles of leadership, of practicing forgiveness, of tithing and giving, of loving their fellow man as themselves, or of simply being obedient? Through an ongoing process of discipleship, parents impart spiritual values to their children that will enable them to succeed in church, in business, in marriage, and in all other aspects of life.

Besides living with your spouse, the greatest challenge to walking out your adult spiritual life in this human body is your family. Have you forgiven past wrongs, let God heal you of resentment and hatred against specific ones, asked forgiveness when you have transgressed against a family member, blessed and encouraged the little ones, honored your parents, and respected your siblings? Do they see and hear Christ Jesus reflected in you? Are you allowing past ruptures in relationships or grudges or squabbles over material possessions to begin affecting the next generation of your family?

Those who have not learned or refused to practice godly principles within their families usually face deep emotional pain that can be carried the rest of their lives. This is an area of great importance to God because He desires for the entire family to be healed in all areas of relationships. Whole families are to be saved, and you, my friend, are the one through whom this transformation may come!

That is a heavy responsibility, but Scripture demonstrates consistently that God's intention is for redemption to come to entire households and extended families. When that occurs, the local church body benefits, as do neighbors, friends, co-workers, and others in the immediate area. The result is a community of regenerated people of God, growing in grace, being generous and giving freely, offering help, supporting the disadvantaged (orphans, widows, the homeless, the hungry, the elderly, the oppressed), walking in integrity, being blessed of God in business, and demonstrating the fruit of the Spirit.

God takes that nucleus of believers and begins building a greater community around it that will call on His name and become His people. You are then in the center of a haven of rest with your family. It brings peace and impacts all areas of your life. You will be a more productive worker or a more profitable business owner, as well as will those who work for you.

One last point about family that I will make is commitment— to the older generations. If God is truly first in your life, you will not neglect your parents or elder brothers and sisters when they get into old age. Read what the Scriptures say about honoring them and loving and caring for them, just as they cared and nurtured you when you were a baby.

Many modern families feel no obligation for the care of their parents and dump them into a nursing home for others to care for. As if that were not bad enough, they neglect them by not visiting and not writing to them. Except for severe medical conditions that may require constant or specialized care, God intended for the Christian family unit to be a cohesive unit of committed, loving members who care for their older as well as their younger ones. This was a commandment of God in His law to the Hebrews, with death as punishment for disobedience! That is how strongly He felt about the matter of honoring your parents, for life.

The *fourth* priority area is your employment: your job, your quality of work, and the people you work together with in achieving goals for the company. The same principles apply to those who are self-employed.

When Adam and Eve were banned from Eden, one of the penalties for their sin was that all mankind would have to work to support themselves. God's ideal environment that He created in Eden for all mankind had been forfeited and would only be reclaimed in Heaven by His elect at the end of the ages. So Adam and Eve had to start finding food, building a home, and living life by their own cleverness and toil, the hard way.

Several thousand years later, we are doing the same, although we have progressed by God's blessing from being hunters and gatherers to being managers of organizations, of technology, and of the environment (crops, water, animals). Each of us still must work and contribute to providing food and protection for ourselves and our families. Here are some examples of why this area is so important.

- Your quality of life depends mainly on your type of work and level of income. That determines the relative degree of peace or pressure you experience from managing your finances, having adequate time for your spouse and family, taking vacations together, and spending time in Bible study and prayer.

    Have you prepared yourself by getting educated, having the right attitude about work, and seeking God's will for where your talents and abilities lie? How can you reasonably support those lower priorities without adequate resources derived from your work? You would be foolish to count on winning lotteries, inheriting wealth, or finding money growing on trees to provide financial support for your life, your spouse, and others in need.

    What is your ability and commitment to tithing from your income? What about giving, which goes beyond the tithe? Your job allows you a certain income, and others besides yourself depend on that resource.

- Your availability for service to the Body of Christ depends to a great degree on how much *time* you spend working. For most people outside of ministry, this area represents the greatest quantity of time spent in a typical day. Try to imagine a man or woman who works for a company for thirty to forty years and then retires. How much quality time have they spent with co-workers, managers, and subordinates during those many years of five-day weeks and eight-hour days? It is a huge amount!

    Time is critical—you can only manage it. You cannot create any more of it, make up for lost time, or afford to squander it foolishly. Your life is but a vapor, and God expects you to get busy being about His business (will) too!

- You have influence on those colleagues and managers whom you work with in the organization. For many people working at a company, there are *more* and *longer-term* relationships in the workplace than at home, in the neighborhood, or at church. Most company employees spend much more time with their colleagues than with their wives and children.

Are you a source of light, a Christian influence, and source of stability? Are you trustworthy, truthful, and dependable? Do you perform your work as unto the Lord or with griping, messiness, poor quality, or boredom? Do your influence on others and quality of work provide you with future opportunities for advancement with greater income? Are co-workers drawn to you, affording opportunities to demonstrate the fruit of the Spirit in your life through daily interaction? God's blessing on your daily life as you walk with Him will allow you to have favor extended from managers who recognize those qualities of honesty, loyalty, commitment, dependability, and other such traits.

Priority number *five* is your church, the local body of believers that you have fellowship with on a regular basis, to whose pastor you are submitted for spiritual oversight and authority, that provides an environment for corporate worship and prayer, and whose vision for outreach ministry you share and participate in. If the previous four priorities have been properly attended to, you will be one of the few members who is spiritually healthy when you arrive to be planted, who can be a consistent giver of resources instead of a consumer, who is financially strong for supporting the various needs of the Body, and who can function with integrity as positions are needed for teaching, administration, and helps. You will walk in wisdom, knowledge, and understanding from God so that people will want or need you to help them, even to disciple them.

But there are those who think they can worship God from home, read the Bible, and watch television ministries for sufficient inclusion in the Body of Christ. Sorry! Those things are good, but there are aspects of collective fellowship and worship that you will miss out on that are very important for each of us.

- *Corporate worship.* You can attain a certain level of individual worship at home, but there is much more to be gained within the corporate worship of a body of believers. When the local church lifts up its collective and sincere voice toward Heaven, God is moved and enters its midst. In Matthew 18:20, Jesus says, "For where two or three are gathered together in My name, there am I in the midst of them." It only takes a minimum of two believers to bring God into the midst. Think of how responsive God must be when He hears one hundred, a thousand, or more believers giving Him praise and magnifying His name on Earth, where He created man to love and to worship Him!

- *Corporate prayer.* Although every believer, individually, has prayer as the direct communication channel to the throne of God (Heb. 4:16), there is *power* in corporate prayer. In Matthew 18:19, Jesus says, "Again I say unto you, That if two of you shall agree on earth as touching any thing that they shall ask, it shall be done for them of My Father which is in Heaven." If you are single or a young person living in a non-Christian household, you need not only the fellowship of other Christians, but you need also prayer partners for prayers of agreement. From my understanding of Scripture, a prayer of agreement with fellow Christians or a spouse is *more effective* than the total prayers of the individuals praying alone about the same issue or need.

- *Outreach ministry.* As I will discuss in a later chapter, faith without works is dead—"kablooey"— pretty much useless! A body of believers, whether a formal church or not, provides believers with opportunities to learn to serve others, to meet needs, and to be discipled in stewardship, leadership, humility, giving, and other Biblical principles of Christian maturity.

You *need* to work in the church—you are the feet and legs of the Kingdom of God on Earth. You can provide gifts and talents that others may lack. Their gifts will complement yours, in turn. Carefully read 1 Corinthians 12:12–27 for how each one is important to the Body of Christ.

We have all been guilty of not valuing all the different individuals God has set within His Body. The Church can marshal the necessary resources to enable its members to reach out to the poor, the drug-addicted, the oppressed, the widow, the crippled, and the other disadvantaged within the community. This is ministry as Jesus practiced it!

Go outside your comfort zone and begin to act on your faith; participate in evangelism, outreach ministries, community charitable programs, and school volunteer programs. It is your responsibility to *act on your faith in God and do the works of Jesus* as clearly described in the books of Matthew through John.

That is how Christians make a dramatic impact on their communities—through their works (and prayers), not through their words. God will help you find sufficient time to be a servant to your fellow man. Your works in the Body of Christ will benefit you directly when you are being rewarded in Heaven with eternal treasures for your service in this life.

- *Being fed and protected as a sheep in the fold of the shepherd.* It is the responsibility of the pastor to seek God's face for a continual fresh flow of His anointing upon his ministry to the Church Body for their nurturing and care. That anointing provides fresh words of spiritual life and the growing use of authority (power) in teaching and preaching, visitation, healing, and deliverance.

In John 21:15–17, Jesus repeatedly stressed to Peter the need to feed the sheep. Apparently, Peter didn't hear the Master with "ears to hear," for Jesus had to say it emphatically three times. Peter was a strong-willed individual who was willing to physically fight for Jesus, as we have learned, but in spiritual matters he could be hardheaded and not easily receive instruction. He must have gotten the message, though, because we later look at his first epistle and are surprised to hear his own words of admonition to the elders of various church bodies scattered around regions north of Israel. In 1 Peter 5:2–3, he said, *"Feed the flock of God* which is among you, taking the oversight thereof, not by constraint, but willingly; not for filthy lucre, but of a ready mind; Neither as being lords over God's heritage, but being ensamples to the flock" (emphasis added).

A great change had occurred in Peter's life since the death of Jesus; the three years of continual discipleship under Jesus, one on one at times and one of twelve at other times, had placed all the right seeds of truth into him. With Jesus gone and Peter's being filled with the Holy Spirit (at Pentecost), Peter had the Holy Spirit to draw out all the truths deposited earlier and to help him walk them out before men. Here he clearly spells out the importance and the responsibility of pastoral care. How ironic for these words to come from Peter!

As Jesus was the Great Shepherd, feeding and protecting the flock, so are today's pastors assuming that role of shepherd. Submit yourself to the care and oversight of a pastor who is following God. It is scriptural, it is life-giving, and it is for your own protection.

If you cannot align yourself with the pastor's vision or if there are no results from his teaching, preaching, and outreach ministries, then go elsewhere! God wants authority in His Body, like that found in an army. Renegades will not be given anointings to minister or responsibility for others, because they themselves are not under spiritual authority.

Remember that there are wolves in sheep's clothing and false prophets within the land and even within the church, waiting to destroy your Bible-based beliefs, deceive you about Biblical doctrine, steal your peace, and keep you from maturing in spiritual matters. In addition, the devourer stalks the Earth like a lion, seeking out those that he can destroy, literally.

There is strength and protection within a body of believers and under a pastor who keeps a vigilant eye for deceivers, false doctrines, and false prophets. Cherish your covering.

Prayer and Fasting: Responsibilities, Benefits, and Callings

If you were going to repair a jet engine, wouldn't you need training and the right tools for that specific make and model of equipment? The same is true for Christians going to battle against evil spirits that oppress and torment, interceding in prayer for another person, or petitioning God for a need to be met. They have to be properly prepared, use the proper tools, and proceed in the right frame of mind, or the job will not get done!

There is unlimited and untapped power available to you through effective prayer and fasting. Don't live beneath your privilege or allow distractions to sidetrack your communications with God and your "putting your body under" when building spiritual strength for Kingdom combat. Otherwise, your answer, message, ministry, or gift (talent) may be delayed or diluted to the point of ineffectiveness.

In the latter days of His Earthly ministry, Jesus had been praying in a place, and one of His disciples realized that he needed instruction about praying. This disciple also knew that John the Baptist had taught his followers how to pray effectively. So he asked Jesus to teach the close group of chosen disciples how to pray.

In Luke 11:2–4, we read what Jesus gave in reply as representative of all the key aspects of general prayer. Study the parts of this example and you will see the steps of an effective prayer. Its components are those critical steps needed for most types of results-oriented prayers: acknowledgment, worship, awareness of God's Word, submission, supplication, dependency, forgiveness, love of fellow man, trust, confidence, and exultation.

Adjust your mind-set before prayer and supplication time so you will surely gain entrance to the presence of God. Therefore, enter into His gates with thanksgiving in your heart, and enter His courts with praise! It is praise and worship of the Father that we were created for, and God responds to His people's thanksgiving and adoration.

Remember that God exists in three persons, or expressions, of identity and operation: Father, Son, and Holy Spirit. Within the totality of His being, which we cannot fully grasp until we are in His presence and know all things, He has made every provision for us from conception to eternity in paradise before Him. Each of us has so many things to be thankful to God for already that it should be easy to spend some quality time in praising Him *before* we begin to ask Him for needs to be met. Worship Him as Creator, the great I Am of the burning bush, the Great Physician, Savior, Lord and Master, the Prince of Peace, the mighty God, Lamb of God, the Alpha and Omega, and our source of life, love, and light.

There are many other titles and names that He is called throughout the Bible, and it is good to keep ourselves built up strong within His many capacities by calling Him those names. He will allow us to come quickly into His presence as we declare His holiness, express our human love for our Creator, and simply adore Him as one individual who is making time for Him.

Look at Hebrews 10:19–23 for a grand assessment of our privilege in prayer.

> Having therefore, brethren, boldness to enter into the holiest by the blood of Jesus, By a new and living way, which he hath consecrated for us, through the veil, that is to say, his flesh; And having an high priest over the house of God; Let us draw near with a true heart in full assurance of faith, having our hearts sprinkled from an evil conscience, and our bodies washed with pure water. Let us hold fast the profes-

sion of our faith without wavering; (for he is faithful that promised).

There are many aspects to prayer, and it is too great a subject to cover in this book. I recommend that you look for some books on prayer by people who live lives of prayer and who don't just write about it. There are also many good books available on types of fasts and the fasting life. While we obey the Father's will for our lives and await the Bridegroom's sudden, unexpected arrival, there are certain principles of prayer and of fasting that I will focus upon.

1. Prayer is our communication channel to God. We have direct communication with God the Father on His throne in Heaven through the work achieved by His Son Jesus. Hebrews 4:14, 16 says, "Seeing then that we have a great high priest, that is passed into the Heavens, Jesus the Son of God, let us hold fast our profession.... Let us therefore come boldly unto the throne of grace, that we may obtain mercy, and find grace to help in time of need."

    It is a tremendous privilege to be able to approach God in prayer directly without a middleman priest and know that He hears every word. Because of Jesus' death and resurrection, He made each of us a royal priest when the veil was torn asunder in the great temple of Jerusalem, before the Holy of Holies. God stated His intention to allow this wholesale change, prophetically through Moses, in ancient times in Exodus 19:6: "And ye shall be unto me *a Kingdom of priests,* and an holy nation" (emphasis added). We can now enter into the presence of God, just as the high priest did annually in the temple's Holy of Holies, because of our re-born and spiritually pure spirits.

    Ephesians 3:12 informs us of our prayer privilege as new creatures in Christ: "In whom we have boldness and access with confidence by the faith of him." Jesus was the ultimate sacrifice, which alleviated the need for any more blood sacrifices. Jesus stands as our High Priest; it is through His name that we enter the presence of God.

Today, whether Jew or Gentile, we who have been born again of the Spirit of God have the same kind of direct access to our Father in Heaven on His throne as a child on Earth does to his own father sitting in the living-room recliner. We should pray in faith, believing for the answer. Remember that Hebrews 11:6 puts the subject of faith directly into our expectations in prayer: "For he that cometh to God must believe that he is, and that he is a rewarder of them that diligently seek him."

2. Prayer moves God when made in alignment with His Word. Don't pray amiss or for selfish motives. James 4:3 says, "Ye ask, and receive not, because ye ask amiss, that ye may consume it upon your lusts." If you pray in alignment with His Word, in agreement with one or two others, with sincerity and with persistence, what is your Father going to do in response? He is a caring Father who loves His children!

3. Do not fail to participate in *corporate prayer* with a body of believers, in addition to your personal prayer time. Hebrews 10:25 speaks to us about the corporate, collective benefit: "Not forsaking the assembling of ourselves together, as the manner of some is; but exhorting one another: and so much the more as ye see the day approaching."

Just as there are huge dividends by participating in corporate worship and corporate fasting, corporate prayer can achieve breakthroughs not only for you but also for the other participants. God responds quickly to two or more believers gathered in His name. Try to imagine the benefit presented by being part of a body of fifty, fifteen hundred, or fifteen thousand sincere believers calling upon God, united in focused prayer for specific needs. I've seen God move through a church body in prayer and do wonderful things that I'm certain would not have happened individually to each one, outside that body.

God is honored when His people come together in His name. He is moved by their prayers, just as He is moved (and welcomed) by their corporate praise. His level or extent of presence in a body and the grace He extends there is greater than the sum of what it would be if He moved on each of the individuals participating.

Take advantage of corporate prayer. God brings about greater or broader results, brings about unity of spirit and cooperation among those who pray together, and He changes you for the better by the experience!

4. We can pray in an unknown tongue (a Heavenly language given to believers by the Holy Spirit when He completely occupies their human spirits and imparts power) when we don't know how to express ourselves or don't know the extent of need. The Holy Spirit marvelously provides this supernatural utterance issuing out of our spirits through our mouths.

Have you received the fullness of the Holy Spirit indwelling as commanded by Jesus of His disciples and as described on the Day of Pentecost for all believers? It is tragic that some churches and entire denominations teach that this wonderful blessing from God after salvation was limited to just the first church, the apostles, and other disciples who were contemporaries of Jesus. God makes this experience available to all mankind since He wants our walk and works to have His power behind them. Take a side path with me for a moment, and let's see what Jesus had to say on this important subject.

> And I will pray the Father, and he shall give you another Comforter, that he may abide with you for ever; Even the Spirit of truth; whom the world cannot receive, because it seeth him not, neither knoweth him: but ye know him; for he dwelleth with you, and shall be in you.... But the Comforter, which is the Holy Ghost, whom the Father will send in my name, he shall teach you all things, and bring all things to your remembrance, whatsoever I have said unto you.
>
> John 14:16–17, 26

Jesus explains that when He is gone from the Earth, the Father will send to all His disciples (followers) the Holy Spirit, to abide both with *and* within them. His Spirit will not be seen or even acknowledged by the unregenerate world in spiritual darkness. The Spirit of God will teach us and remind us of Jesus' words, which we have in Scripture from the creation.

> But when the Comforter is come, whom I will send unto you from the Father, even the Spirit of truth, which proceedeth from the Father, he shall testify of me: And ye also shall bear witness, because ye have been with me from the beginning.
>
> John 15:26–27

This passage says the Holy Spirit will come and reside in the believer who seeks Him, and will testify of Jesus. How can the Holy Spirit speak to man about Jesus? Answer: through the vocal cords and mouths of believers whom He has filled with His presence! As He gives the utterance and as we are yielded, He speaks wonderful praises to worship and adore the Son of God, the Lamb of God who was slain for us before the foundations of the world were laid. We don't understand the language, but God and Jesus do as they sit upon their thrones in Heaven.

Jesus then told the disciples that they would be able to confirm to people that this new and profound experience was precisely as Jesus had said when He walked the Earth. They had witnessed His teachings, and they would then witness the outpouring of the Holy Spirit on the Day of Pentecost.

> Nevertheless I tell you the truth; it is expedient for you that I go away: for if I go not away, the Comforter will not come unto you; but if I depart, I will send him unto you.... Howbeit when he, the Spirit of truth is come, he will guide you into all truth: for he shall not speak of himself; but whatsoever he shall hear, that shall he speak: and he will shew you things to come. He shall glorify me: for he shall receive of mine, and shall show it unto you. All things that the Father hath are mine: there-

fore said I, that he shall take of mine, and shall show it unto you.

John 16:7, 13–15

This is very revealing about some of the Holy Spirit's purposes for indwelling believers. He will *guide* us in truth for all of our remaining lives. What He *hears* or is told *in Heaven,* He will speak it on Earth. (Remember how He speaks on Earth.) He will *speak of future events*. He will *glorify* Jesus. He will *show* us, demonstrate, and make manifest the things provided by Christ Jesus.

What are those things? I think they are gifts of the Spirit, anointings, dreams and visions, signs and wonders, offices, callings, administrations, prayer needs, and all of the other marvelous spiritual gifts from God that are described and shown throughout the Gospels and the remainder of the New Testament writings. These all issue from God and operate in believers through the orchestration of the Holy Spirit.

In these Scriptures, Jesus peels open for us some insights into the spirit realm and its bounty for His Body of believers, all under the direction of His Spirit within us. How hungry are you for His Spirit and the deeper gifts of His provision?

Let's look now at another Scriptural passage: "Then said Jesus to them again, Peace be unto you: as my Father hath sent me, even so send I you. And when he had said this, he breathed on them, and saith unto them, Receive ye the Holy Ghost" (John 20:21–22). Jesus had risen from the dead, victorious, and visited His disciples to finish His direct input into their lives. He told them that He was sending them out into the world, just as His Father had sent Him to the world to be the Redeemer of mankind. He did not intend to send them out without the proper covering; He commanded them to be filled with the Holy Ghost, which they received at Pentecost after His ascension into Heaven.

Acts 1:2, 4–5, 8; 2:1–4, 11, 16–19, 33, and 38 need to be read, written upon the heart, meditated upon, and stood upon for both the fulfillment of Jesus' promise and the tremendous power that was imparted to believers for them to unleash upon the darkness of the world. These verses are the central Biblical reference to the same outpouring of His Spirit today upon those who hunger for a deeper walk with God and yield to His Spirit. Don't allow doubters, mockers, religious spirits, traditions of men, or unbelief to keep you from partaking of His great gift.

Finally, Jude 20 says, "But ye, beloved, building up yourselves on your most holy faith, praying in the Holy Ghost." Here Jude links being strong in faith with praying in the Spirit. There are supernatural things that occur when God's people pray in the Spirit, for the benefit of both the one praying and the object of the prayer!

The Holy Spirit knows precisely what is needed in prayer, what the Word has to say about it, and how to make the petition clearly stated to God the Father on faith in that Word. First Corinthians 14:14 says, "For if I pray in an unknown tongue, my *spirit* prayeth" (emphasis added). He bypasses our mind so that it cannot interfere with the upward prayer that is precisely tailored to the need.

Look at Paul's writings to the church in Rome: "Likewise the Spirit also helpeth our infirmities: for we know not what we should pray for as we ought: but the Spirit itself maketh intercession for us with groanings which cannot be uttered. And he that searcheth the hearts knoweth what is the mind of the Spirit, because he maketh intercession for the saints according to the will of God" (Rom. 8:26–27).

This marvelous gift of tongues and groanings allows us to never reach a dead end when praying. The Holy Spirit will always speak to God in perfect alignment with the Word of Truth and with just the message needed. He will speak to the Father out of our innermost beings (where He resides) and convey all necessary information, exactly as the need requires. What an asset the Holy Spirit is to us, extending our expression of praise and worship, intercession, or petitions to the Father beyond the human constraints of body and soul!

5. Fasting added to prayer is like a tritium trigger added to a thermonuclear bomb: it increases its explosiveness by a tremendous

amount. The act of fasting puts the body and soul under the dominion of the spirit of a man. It strengthens the inner man through continual meditation upon and reading of God's Word. Not just abstinence from food, but also sexual abstinence helps the body and soul (with its basic human desires) to lay aside typical desires and come under submission to the spirit.

How much more effective is the prayer of a person who has been fasting and praying about an issue than one who has just been praying? King David said, "I humbled my soul with fasting" (Ps. 35:15) and later commented, I "chastened my soul with fasting" (Ps. 69:10). These words are from the heart of a man whose heart was after God and through whose lineage the Son of God, the lion of the tribe of Judah, later emerged.

Jesus told his perplexed disciples in Matthew 17:21 that some kinds of strong evil spirits (a strongman) go out of an oppressed person only after prayer *and* fasting. Of course, faith in God's Word and the authority that Jesus delegated to disciples have to be in operation in order for success to occur, just as in any spiritual endeavor. The disciples had been unable to cast out the strong ruling spirit in the lunatic boy by prayer alone, and He pointed out their weakness, which they had not previously encountered in deliverance ministry.

Anytime you face a bigger mountain or greater force, use fasting together with prayer as your irresistible force. Fasting, together with prayer, becomes a mighty force because the body and soul are forced (brought into submission) to align with what the spirit is focused upon.

There are very few distractions and obstacles in the way of those who have been fasting and praying for the needs of someone else or for themselves. The flesh and mind are both submitted to the spirit, the Word of Truth is bubbling up fresh each day, and the spirit is praising God with great joy. Use that extra firepower available through fasting to secure the answer to prayer!

There are two good examples of fasting and prayer in the Bible that reflect the intense situations requiring fasting to reach God and obtain answers. The outcome in these two instances of prayer by shepherds of men determined the physical life or spiritual death of millions of people.

- Moses, Exodus 32–34: After Moses had been upon Mount Sinai for forty days and nights talking with God about the future nation of Israel, the commandments to be given to the people, and the details about the design and materials for the tabernacle of the congregation, he came down from the mountain to find the people naked and worshipping before a golden calf. Before God destroyed all these stiff-necked people, Moses went back up the mountain for another forty days and nights to intercede on behalf of his people and their destiny. His prolonged period of fasting, coupled with continuous intercessory prayer before God in the darkness of the cloud cover while reminding Him of the Word of Truth He swore to Abraham, moved God. "And the Lord repented of the evil which he thought to do unto his people" (Exod. 32:14).

  Had Moses not availed himself of the spiritual strength achieved through prolonged fasting, I'm not sure that he would have successfully persuaded God to change His mind. God already had a plan B in mind to implement after destroying the Israelites (Exod. 32:10).

- Jesus, Matthew 4: Jesus was on the verge of starting His ministry, which would forever change the world and bring salvation to all mankind, not just to Israel. He had been baptized in water (born of water) and filled with the Holy Spirit, and His Father had said that it was now time to start His Earthly ministry.

  At such a critical stage of His life, with the weight of mankind's salvation upon Him, He was ready to be tempted by the enemy and proven strong. What would you have done? Jesus chose *to fast* for forty days and nights to ensure maximum spiritual strength against the wiles of the devil. It was successful! He never yielded one inch of spiritual ground or lost His credibility as the true Son of God, He never yielded to His fleshly desires, and His authority over evil did not diminish one iota. He came forth from this test having validated His authority and standing as the Sinless One, the only one worthy to be the ultimate sacrifice for all man, for all sin, for all times.

6. Be careful to pray *in Jesus' name* (only) since that is the only name under Heaven by which we have access to the Father and by whose blood we are saved. Jesus tells us in John 10:9, "I am the door: by me if any man enter in, he shall be saved." John 14:6, 13–14 gives the words of Jesus as He is concluding His teaching to His disciples just prior to His crucifixion. He speaks first to Thomas and then to Philip before speaking to the group of disciples: "Jesus saith unto him, I am the way, the truth, and the life: no man cometh unto the Father, but by me.... And whatsoever ye shall ask in my name, that will I do, that the Father may be glorified in the Son. If ye shall ask any thing in my name, I will do it."

There is no Biblical basis for praying to any other name—not to angels, Mary, saints, priests, Buddha, Allah, or to any of the original disciples and apostles. Praying to any name other than Jesus avails nothing!

The same is true concerning the use of relics, prayer beads, icons, crucifixes, repetitious prayers, medallions, crossing the heart, chants, mind-altering drugs, kissing of relics and stones, figurines, and amulets. These are typically the result of religious traditions of man evolving over the centuries and may even have religious spirits attached to their use. They will hinder, at a minimum, and possibly block your prayers from ascending to God. Any religious spirits associated with these "prayer aids" will certainly seek to delude the person using them into thinking that the object or other aid to prayer was critical to gaining a successful answer, thus reinforcing the use of the crutch when praying again.

Read the Book of Life yourself and learn what instructions, rules, laws, and penalties God assigned to the use of graven images or substitutes/aids of any type. He did not want anyone to try to make any type of physical object to hang on the wall, affix to the body, or set within the house to represent Him. I mention this because we have homes with paintings, figurines, crucifixes, and holiday decorations and ornaments representing Jesus—some showing Him as a baby in the manger, some as being crucified on the cross, some as being a young man teaching on the hillside, and some showing Him holding a lamb as a shepherd. Most show Him as a blue- or brown-eyed Caucasian, but very few show Him as a representative black-eyed Jewish Middle Easterner of that time period.

As humans, we are not capable of describing God. We have never seen Him; the Bible does not describe Him for us; and our unregenerate mind is incapable of fashioning any painting, drawing, statue, or image of Him that is true to life and pleasing to Him.

Which way do you think of Jesus or want your children to grow up thinking of Him? None of us know anything about Jesus except what He has revealed to us in His Word. Apparently, God did not want man to have any specific (and wrong) image in mind when thinking, praying, or praising Him. He knew what man was capable of; and He knew that people would argue about His features, different cultures would ascribe various facial features that resembled their own, and some religious groups might go to battle over certain depictions of God or His Son. I can see why God forbade the representation of Himself by the people.

We do not know what He looked like during His life on Earth because God chose not to tell us! But we do know that Jesus presently sits at the right hand of the Father in Heaven, ready to Advocate, or intercede, with the Father on our behalves when we come to Him in prayer. I am not going to think of Him as a baby in the manger, a boy in the temple, or a shepherd in the field, even though He was all those things. When I enter into prayer, He is clearly shown in my mind's eye as the royal King, our Advocate, our High Priest, the Lamb of God who put all things under His feet and sits in royalty on the throne beside the Father. He is the one who speaks on my behalf, who has answers to every situation and disease I face, and Who one day will be the only one worthy of opening and reading from the Book of Life at the great day of judgment.

Any other mental image of Him is beneath our privilege when coming into His presence through prayer before God the Father. Shake off religious traditions and thinking, superstitions, and belief in luck—expand your opportunities for results in prayer!

7. Pray out loud. There is power in the *spoken word,* as demonstrated throughout the Bible and exemplified by the teaching and ministry of Jesus. Unleash that power! Do not merely think through your prayer to God but enjoy the privilege of vocally coming into His presence, making your petitions known, respectfully reminding Him of His Word that you are standing upon, and laying your needs and intercessions before Him on the altar.

God imparted unique authority and power to the human voice He created, so unleash that power when talking to God. When you pray, remember to get into a private, distraction-free place where your body, soul, and spirit can all focus upon the living God. Kneel or bow before Him to show respect and honor for His holiness, His love for you, and His granting access to you to His throne room to communicate your prayers and praises.

From experience, I can tell you that your body will resist yielding, submitting, kneeling, or bowing. It will tire easily during earnest prayer, so get as comfortable as feasible. Your soul (mind, will, emotions) will tend to be easily distracted, so shut out all sounds of music, television, thoughts of your day's activities, memories of the baby crying, recent loss of job, bills due, and other such things. It is imperative to have focused, quality effort in touching God in prayer.

Unfortunately, many people who do not commit to an active prayer life relegate their prayer time to when they fall into bed tired at the end of the day. They pray *silently in their thoughts,* quietly lying in bed, and usually fall asleep without achieving breakthrough and obtaining results. Is that effective prayer? Is

God moved by that kind of prayer and willing to intervene to bring about change?

It is the sound of our voices, His creation, that arouses His attention. It is the sincerity and determination of our prayers that bring results from on high. Here is an example of a man who heard some bad news about his health from a messenger, immediately prayed to God in the right attitude and environment, and obtained an extension of life before the messenger even got over halfway out the residence's courtyard: 2 Kings 20:1–7.

8. At every opportunity after your prayer time is completed, spend some quiet time *waiting* upon the Lord. The disciples of Jesus were told to pray fervently and *to wait* for the gift of the Holy Spirit at Pentecost after Jesus' ascension. David said in several Psalms' verses how important it was to wait upon the Lord, stating that He would lead him in truth and teach him His ways. He was willing to wait all day upon God to hear Him speak and act on his behalf. For example, Psalm 25:5 says, "Lead me in thy truth, and teach me: for thou art the God of my salvation; on thee do I wait all the day; and Psalm 27:14 declares, "Wait on the Lord: be of good courage, and he shall strengthen thine heart: wait, I say, on the Lord."

What if you miss what He has to say or show to you after you've talked to Him? He speaks into your spirit through that still, small voice, and you need to be quiet in environment, mind, and body to hear Him clearly. Keep still and do not allow anything to distract your mind. Anticipate hearing His voice. The enemy may try to interject thoughts to cause you to lose focus, but resist the devil and he'll flee from you!

Some of my most treasured times in prayer have been in those quiet times afterward when I waited upon Him and He began to speak to me. Sometimes His words were pertaining to my needs or requests for others that I had just presented to Him. At other times, what He had to say was unrelated to what I had been praying about. Occasionally He instructed me to write down the words He was going to say.

Those are sacred times alone with your God, your Creator, and cannot be equaled by any substitute experience. Don't fail to give Him an opportunity to talk to you after you've talked to Him!

Stewardship: Principles Involved

The use of the word *stewardship* is rare in today's secular society *and* in the Body of Christ because of several factors.

- It implies accountability of ownership or use.
- It does not imply permanence of ownership or use.
- It implies profitable use.
- We (or the marketplace) like to determine the value of what we own.

These are not popular notions; we want to own or have clear title to things, have the freedom to do with them as we want and when we want, and may not want to do anything more with them than setting them around for us to look at and enjoy. The less value that we assign to an object, the less potential that we see in it for gain.

However, these natural desires to work to possess things and then to do as we please with them are not the desires that emerge from a heart that has died to self in a prayer closet and that God is transforming into the image of Jesus Christ. The mature believer learns from Scripture and from listening to God's Spirit that he is merely a holder, a steward, of everything God places within his hands. God created and owns all things, and it is He who places them in our hands to build His Body, the living temple of God.

Psalm 24:1 covers a lot of territory when it declares, "The earth is the Lord's, and the fullness thereof; the world, and they that dwell therein." This includes even the gems and precious metals that the unregenerate lust for: "The silver is mine, and the gold is mine, saith the Lord of hosts" (Hag. 2:8).

As bond servants of Christ, we must change our thinking to realize that all things are temporary, come to us from our Father, and are to be valued by God as He sees them worthy of use; He will direct us in using them, selling them, or giving them away to others. One other very sobering thought is that He will hold us accountable at the Judgment Seat of Christ for our handling of what He has given to us and our submission to His will in these objects, treasures (gems and precious metals), funds, property, pets, and other possessions. God gives us things to sow into His Kingdom on Earth and to help others to become strong members of His Body. It is yet another key area of the believer's walk with God that requires a submissive heart, a hearing ear, and feet and hands to accomplish His purposes.

Before going further into the subject of stewardship, let's see a few things that Jesus had to say on the subject. He had a lot to say because He knew that *many believers* would fall short when they stood before Him for their lives as believers to be evaluated.

1. Luke 12:42–49 (NASB):

> And the Lord said, "Who then is the faithful and sensible steward, whom his master will put in charge of his servants, to give them their rations at the proper time? Blessed is that slave whom his master finds so doing when he comes. Truly I say to you, that he will put him in charge of all his possessions. But if that slave says in his heart, 'My master will be a long time in coming,' and begins to beat the slaves, both men and women, and to eat and drink and get drunk; the master of that slave will come on a day when he does not expect him, and at an hour he does not know, and will cut him in pieces, and assign him a place with the unbelievers. And that slave who knew his master's will and did not get ready or act

in accord with his will, shall receive many lashes, but the one who did not know it, and committed deeds worthy of a flogging, will receive but few. And from everyone who has been given much shall much be required; and to whom they entrusted much, of him they will ask all the more. I have come to cast fire upon the earth; and how I wish it were already kindled!"

There are a significant number of stewardship principles revealed in this parable that Jesus gave. First, the degree to which a servant pleases the master by how he handles his responsibilities determines if that servant is considered faithful and sensible. That servant will be blessed (rewarded) for his obedience. The good servant is found *doing* (present tense) the master's will when the master suddenly appears. The faithful servant gets authority over all the master's possessions because he did exactly what was required of him, and he did it well till the end.

The unfaithful and unrighteous servant, though, gets treated far differently when the master shows up unexpectedly. He is treated harshly, his authority is taken away, and he is assigned a place *with the unbelievers*. This servant had been a believer and knew the master's will but chose to do what he wanted with the master's property. Jesus then stated strongly that He will require a great deal of accountability from those who are given much authority regarding His possessions. To the faithful/obedient, much more will be given/rewarded.

Why did He then wish that judgment fire was already kindled upon Earth? The answer: so His judgment fire would already be burning up all the chaff, wood, hay, and stubble in our lives! Only the things, or works, of everlasting value will survive His fire of judgment. Today He uses holy fire to purify His people, who are like precious metals, with various impurities, taken from the earth. One day in the future, His holy fire will be the consuming force that destroys all unrighteous works, motives, and thoughts for eternity.

2. Matthew 25:14–34:

> For the Kingdom of Heaven is as a man traveling into a far country, who called his own servants, and delivered unto them his goods. And unto one he gave five talents, to another two, and to another one; to every man according to his several ability; and straightway took his journey. Then he that had received the five talents went and traded with the same, and made them other five talents. And likewise he that had received two, he also gained other two. But he that had received one went and digged in the earth, and hid his lord's money. After a long time the lord of those servants cometh, and reckoneth with them. And so he that had received five talents came and brought other five talents, saying, Lord, thou deliveredst unto me five talents: behold, I have gained beside them five talents more. His lord said unto him, Well done, thou good and faithful servant: thou has been faithful over a few things, I will make thee ruler over many things: enter thou into the joy of thy lord. He also that had received two talents came and said, Lord, thou deliveredst unto me two talents: behold, I have gained two other talents beside them. His lord said unto him, Well done, good and faithful servant; thou has been faithful over a few things, I will make thee ruler over many things: enter thou into the joy of thy lord. Then he which had received the one talent came and said, Lord, I knew thee that thou art an hard man, reaping where thou has not sown, and gathering where thou hast not strawed: And I was afraid, and went and hid thy talent in the earth: lo, there thou hast that is thine. His lord answered and said unto him, Thou wicked and slothful servant, thou knewest that I reap where I sowed not, and gather where I have not strawed: Thou oughtest therefore to have put my money to the exchangers, and then at my coming I should have received mine own with usury. Take therefore the talent from him, and give it unto him which hath

ten talents. For unto every one that hath [increase] shall be given, and he shall have abundance: but from him that hath not [increase] shall be taken away even that which he hath. And cast ye the unprofitable servant into outer darkness: there shall be weeping and gnashing of teeth. When the Son of man shall come in his glory, and all the holy angels with him, then shall he sit upon the throne of his glory: And before him shall be gathered all nations: and he shall separate them one from another, as a shepherd divideth his sheep from the goats: And he shall set the sheep on his right hand, but the goats on the left. Then shall the King say unto them on his right hand, Come, ye blessed of my Father, inherit the Kingdom prepared for you from the foundation of the world.

This longer parable doesn't leave anything to doubt about God's attitude toward believers' responsibilities of stewardship in His Kingdom on Earth and the accountability imposed at the Judgment Seat of Christ for how well or how poorly His possessions were handled. What can we glean from this great teaching?

- The servants were the master's family, part of his household, not strangers or unbelievers. These are today's Christians, part of the family of God, to whom some are given educational opportunities, ministries, businesses, families, spiritual gifts, property, jobs, inheritances, and many other assets.

- The master apportioned a different value of his property to each of the servants. The servants did not all receive the same possession to be responsible for. God may know that one person would not be capable of managing for Him or mature enough to be blessed with the responsibility and taxes on ten thousand acres of beachfront southern California property. However, that one could be given a local job with the opportunity to reach others for the Kingdom of God and to grow into management with all its benefits and perks.

To another might be given a home and family to shepherd, protect, provide for, disciple, and win for the Kingdom of God. To another He might give a little goat. Hopefully, that person would not be offended by the blessing and would nurture the little goat into maturity, obtain milk from it, rent it out for grass and weed elimination, sell the milk for a profit, make some goat cheese, and pay tithes on all the income from this one little goat. That would be an example of leveraging what God gives into a much greater asset for the master.

• Each servant had to make a decision about how to handle the responsibility given. This is an active process of decision-making, rather than a passive acceptance of some new possession to add to the others accumulated. It was up to them, individually, to decide how and when they would work to increase the value of their master's property. This emphasizes works in our lives, putting actions to our faith.

The first two servants of this parable went into the marketplace, and each doubled the value of his master's property. Although the value was different and the gain different, these two wise servants were actively working to make their master a profit on his investment in them. Unfortunately, the third servant put the master's investment in a jar and buried it, hiding it from others and keeping it out of the realm of profitable gain. Jesus said the same thing about believers being a light, like a candle. If you put a candle under a basket and hide the light, others cannot find it and benefit from the light.

• There will be a day of reckoning for all believers. At the Judgment Seat of Christ, their works, their stewardship, their thoughts and motives, and their lives since becoming believers will be examined and rewarded (or punished) accordingly. Until we pass this "final examination" before Christ, we have only the *hope* of life eternal in Heaven.

The master in this parable called all the servants together and dispensed justice to each one. Two pleased the master, and he rewarded them greatly for being diligent to work for him in gaining a profitable increase for his investment. Unfortunately, the slothful servant who did not work responsibly for his master, who let the fear of failure paralyze him, and who did not fear his master's accountability requirements more than his own fears was severely punished. He had not exercised enough common sense to go to his local bank and merely deposit the money and earn some minimal interest. This would have provided some small gain to the master, and I'm sure that there would have been some equivalent measure of reward given for the slight gain.

God requires profitable servants who put Him first in all things, who actively work on His behalf, who show an increase from what they are originally given, and who directly benefit the Kingdom during this Earthly life. The greater the increase, the greater the reward awaiting the believer.

Don't be naïve and think that God will reward all believers the same. Jesus clearly explains that this is not the case. Just as the original investments by the master were variable and the gains by the servants variable, so are the proportions of rewards and punishments by Jesus variable. But He is just in His review of believers' works, and His judgments are true. Those rewards and punishments given will be eternal, as the Scripture above illustrates very clearly.

The subject of righteous stewardship also calls for some examination of the current widespread message of prosperity and wealth accumulation that pervades the Body of Christ. Let's look at *Jesus' own words* on this subject so that we don't deal in conjecture, traditions of men, doctrines of error, greed, or carnal efforts to justify working to get rich.

God does want His people to prosper, and there are many examples of His blessing upon those who are faithful stewards and who are obedient to Him. However, there is a distorted message of prosperity that is very popular among some ministries, which is not based on works of faith, reward for faithful stewardship, or God's true blessing. That message reeks of wealth accumulation, materialism, pride, arrogance, pomp, and ceremony. We will look at that message too.

1. Please read Luke 12:15–34 in its entirety. This is an excellent teaching by Jesus in which He hits at the heart of wealth, the relative value of possessions, choices to make in this life, and consequences for having your heart set on material things. Several of these verses stand out.

   a. Verse 15: "And he said unto them, Take heed, and beware of covetousness: for a man's life consisteth not in the abundance of the things which he possesseth."

      Do you covet recognition among peers, wealth to reflect your relative success, or an image of prosperity? Can you discriminate between a really strong desire and covetousness? What is the motive behind the strong desire for those things?

   b. Verses 18–19: "And he said, This will I do: I will pull down my barns, and build greater.... And I will say to my soul, Soul, thou hast much goods laid up for many years; take thine ease, eat, drink, and be merry."

      In this example the man whose inner thoughts are revealed in these verses met with a terrible fate because he was self-serving, thinking and planning only for himself. He had barns already overflowing with goods, yet he wanted to accumulate even more for himself. It never entered his mind to liquidate the excess and give to those in need around him. He wanted to put his confidence in those goods to sustain him for many, many years to come. His eyes had gotten off of spiritual values and this man had no eternity-based mentality. He considered himself self-sufficient for this temporal life.

Most of us wouldn't be quite so obvious about our selfish goal of heaping up possessions for ourselves. I can almost hear the moths chewing away and the rust flaking off the metal of his stored goods as I read this account!

c. Verse 21: "So is he that layeth up treasure for himself, and is not rich toward God."

Are we laying up treasures in Heaven, or are we consumed with laying them up here in a world of darkness, enjoying them for a very short time (remember the vapor analogy) and then going into eternity without comfort?

d. Verse 31: "But rather seek ye the Kingdom of God; and all these things shall be added unto you."

The wise man who seeks spiritual depth in his walk with God and whose desire is upon spiritual gifts and daily discourse with God will be producing a profitable return on God's possessions, giving him untold rewards, treasures, and perks in Heaven for all eternity. Earthly needs such as food, shelter, clothing, and companionship will all be supplied by our Father while we are working on His behalf as faithful stewards.

e. Verse 34: "For where your treasure is, there will your heart be also."

Jesus reminds us that covetousness is sin and then proceeds to address the more subtle aspects of greed and excess that are "heartworms" damaging the soul and causing the mind to be deluded into thinking about *everything but* being a laborer in the harvest. His central focus to his audience was a challenge: Where is your treasure? He knew that if we have our affections set on luxury homes, luxury cars, people deferring to us, public recognition, being highly esteemed, and a general lifestyle of luxury, we will be *in poverty with God,* not working to store up eternal treasures in Heaven. He did tell us that if we have our priorities aligned with God's, the Earthly needs will all be met.

2. Matthew 6:19–21 NLT: "Don't store up treasures here on earth, where moths eat them and rust destroys them, and where thieves break in and steal. Store your treasures in Heaven, where moths and rust cannot destroy, and thieves do not break in and steal. Wherever your treasure is, there the desires of your heart will also be."

I know of and have seen many Christian people, including some ministers, who spend fortunes on designer clothes, alter their natural appearance by plastic surgery, indulge their multiple vanities, and make it a point to always present an image of ultimate success when in the public eye. How much of that excess spending could have gone into building orphanages, addiction-recovery centers, medical clinics in poor neighborhoods, and supporting outreach ministries that make significant improvements in people's lives for God's Kingdom?

Instead of a $400,000 Rolls Royce sitting in the driveway (and probably someone to drive it), why not buy ten $40,000 cars, use one, and give the other nine away to those who don't have *any* car? How much value would you place on a new, reliable car in a family of six that has an old high-mileage car that barely gets them to church? How many single mothers can't work because they don't have a car, decent clothes for work, or adequate food for their children?

I feel certain that I know what Jesus would have to say about many contemporary attitudes of self-serving spending, accumulation (not sharing) of wealth, maintaining a status level, being image-conscious, and wanting to be recognized as successful by friends, neighbors, and colleagues. In the Church today, this many times takes the form of "being blessed" and "prospering" when trying to justify the excesses of spending and an extravagant lifestyle.

3. Luke 16:19–26 NASB:

> Now there was a rich man, and he habitually dressed in purple and fine linen, joyously living in splendor every day. And a poor man named Lazarus was laid at his gate, covered with sores, and longing to be fed with the crumbs which were falling from the rich man's table; besides, even the dogs were coming and licking his sores. Now the poor man died and was carried away by the angels to Abraham's bosom; and the rich man also died and was buried. In Hades he lifted up his eyes, being in torment, and saw Abraham far away and Lazarus in his bosom. And he cried out and said, "Father Abraham, have mercy on me, and send Lazarus so that he may dip the tip of his finger in water and cool off my tongue, for I am in agony in this flame." But Abraham said, "Child, remember that during your life you received your good things, and likewise Lazarus bad things; but now he is being comforted here, and you are in agony. And besides all this, between us and you there is a great chasm fixed, so that those who wish to come over from here to you will not be able, and that none may cross over from there to us."

Ouch! This true story by Jesus steps on all our collective toes! We pass by people all the time and usually fail to see their needs because we're not looking for them. Here we learn of a wealthy man who was very image-conscious and used his wealth to routinely polish that image. A very poor man who couldn't walk and was covered with infected sores was laid at his gate, too weak to fend off the nasty feral dogs that licked the exudate from his sores. (I'm sure he was thankful that they didn't eat him.) The rich man ignored the poor man, feeling no responsibility to help him in the least by getting him some basic medical care, clothing him properly for his state, or even feeding him by having his servants give him crumbs from his sumptuous dining table.

Unfortunately, the penalty for this kind of crass behavior toward the poor man at his gate proved eternally severe for the rich man. He found himself doomed in a place of torment, unable to obtain relief. When he made a request of Abraham for water, we see that he still looked down on the poor man as one whom Abraham should send to fetch his water and bring it to him. The rot of blatant materialism had so eaten his soul that he didn't realize his hopeless condition of torment relative to the true family of God across the gulf.

At this point, let's see what Jesus said about the principles of Christlike behavior that this rich man would not practice during his Earthly life. We will see that these principles are not situational, circumstantial, culturally or racially excused, or overlooked in Jesus' examination of our lives at His judgment seat. They are absolute and reflect precisely the attitude of our Lord, who will be our judge. Keep in mind as you read this passage that this is Jesus bringing together all of His Body, including you and me. The sinners who never accepted Him are not present at this gathering. Instead, they face the Father at His great White Throne Judgment.

> But when the Son of Man comes in his glory, and all the angels with him, then he will sit upon his glorious throne. All the nations will be gathered in his presence, and he will separate them as a shepherd separates the sheep from the goats. He will place the sheep at his right hand and the goats at his left. Then the King will say to those on the right, "Come, you who are blessed by my Father, inherit the Kingdom prepared for you from the foundation of the world. For I was

hungry, and you fed me. I was thirsty, and you gave me a drink. I was a stranger, and you invited me into your home. I was naked, and you gave me clothing. I was sick, and you cared for me. I was in prison, and you visited me."

Then these righteous ones will reply, "Lord, when did we ever see you hungry and feed you? Or thirsty and give you something to drink? Or a stranger and show you hospitality? Or naked and give you clothing? When did we ever see you sick or in prison, and visit you?" And the King will tell them, "I assure you, when you did it to one of the least of these my brothers and sisters, you were doing it to me!"

Then the King will turn to those on the left and say, "Away with you, you cursed ones, into the eternal fire prepared for the Devil and his demons! For I was hungry, and you didn't feed me. I was thirsty, and you didn't give me anything to drink. I was a stranger, and you didn't invite me into your home. I was naked, and you gave me no clothing. I was sick and in prison, and you didn't visit me."

Then they will reply, "Lord, when did we ever see you hungry or thirsty or a stranger or naked or sick or in prison, and not help you?" And he will answer, "I assure you, when you refused to help the least of these my brothers and sisters, you were refusing to help me." And they will go away into eternal punishment, but the righteous will go into eternal life.

Matthew 25:31–46 (NLT)

It is easy to see that the majority of believers presented before the Lord were *not prepared* for this degree of examination. The good stewards had been obedient and productive in their stewardship but had not truly realized that what they were doing with their fellow man was literally as "unto the Lord."

The goats had no clue; they were not obedient to His commandments and proved to be unfaithful stewards, short of good works and lacking the giving, loving nature of God that is required to reach out to others. We see in another passage of Scripture where the same goats had some in their midst who tried to justify their eternal reward by stating to Jesus that they had healed the sick and cast out devils in His name. Their end was described to be the same as this group standing here.

In contrast to the goats, the sheep had diligently prepared for this occasion by investing their resources to serve God and their fellow man; yet they had been naïve about the scope and depth of reality in bearing fruit for the Kingdom of God. They were very focused on their fellow man, and their motives were pure: love of their fellow man and obedience to their loving God. They were rewarded for their obedience to the will of God. Selfless, they had placed others' needs above their own desires for hoarding possessions, time, and money for themselves.

Unfortunately for the other group on the left, their hearts and motives were judged to be impure, unrighteous, unloving, and selfish. They, too, were not prepared for this level of detailed examination of their works. They had no good works or fruit to show in their lives toward their fellow man. They had not been faithful to obey the Word of Truth. Remember what Jesus told us about the new commandment? John 13:34–35 states: "A new commandment I give unto you, That ye love one another, as I have loved you, that ye also love one another. By this shall all men know that ye are my disciples, if ye have love one to another."

4. John 2:13–17 NIV:

> When it was almost time for the Jewish Passover, Jesus went up to Jerusalem. In the temple courts he found men selling cattle, sheep and doves, and others sitting at tables exchanging money. So he made a whip out of cords, and drove all from the temple area, both sheep and cattle; he scattered the coins of the money changers and overturned their tables. To those who sold doves he said, "Get these out of here! How dare you turn my Father's house into a market!"

Jesus was so incensed about the wholesale commercialism of sacrificial rites by the temple priests that in His righteous anger, He created a corded whip and physically drove out the commercial dealers from the temple. I'm sure the priests watched this spectacle from a safe distance within the temple, not daring to say anything against this righteous man who stood upon the principles of the Word of God.

Why were there so many animals in the temple area? There were abundant animals present in the temple because the priests had become opportunists greedy for money, and the people had become spiritually lazy. They no longer were choosing their own sacrificial animals from their households and bringing them to God's house; they could buy one on the spot and not have to bother with bringing it to the temple.

Why were there so many doves being sold, and why the need for money changers? The hearts of many of the people had turned toward what was the *least level* of commitment required, which was a cheap dove to offer to the priests for a sacrifice. (God had approved doves for sacrifice so that *poor* people could afford to meet the requirement of a proper clean-animal sacrifice.) Other animals to sacrifice cost significantly more, so they took the least costly item on the approved list, even if they could afford the greater sacrifice.

The money changers were needed because the people were buying sacrifices, no longer bringing them from their own stock. They expected change, and the money changers probably charged a fee for the convenience, like our bank ATMs today. I imagine that the wealthy and politically connected priesthood allocated places in the temple areas for favored money-changer friends, charging them a booth rental fee in return.

Does this scene look like the present-day church: lazy flock, greedy ministers, least commitment necessary, insincere hearts, and growing bureaucracy? Are we bold enough to remove those things that have gradually crept into the house of God and fueled someone's greed or vanity? This subject should be a matter of prayer for the Body as a whole, not just for each ministry and local church. We will be held accountable for our stewardship of God's possessions that He has entrusted to us, as well as judged for our motives, desires, and thoughts behind the possessions and our use of them.

Once again, ouch! We believers have allowed materialism and commerce to establish themselves in the Church Body, and we must be diligent to root them out. Many television ministries seem more focused on what they are selling (vitamins, nutritional supplements, holy-water vials, exercise tapes, anointing-oil vials and "special" vessels, prayer handkerchiefs, CDs and DVDs, their latest books, and on and on) than on getting people saved, baptized in water, and filled with the Holy Spirit. It appears that they treat ministry as a money-making business: the more successful, the more money. Much of this unholy commerce is done under the broad guise of "prosperity."

Some of the best (most successful?) ministers at the top work the crowd as well as a good carnival barker! Vanity and foolishness are rampant during services, even during worship and the message. Often the faithful are made to echo back certain choice words throughout the service, high-five each other all around, repeat certain phrases a specific number of times, and engage in other types of soulish behavior that distracts from truly honoring God's presence corporately when His anointing should be flowing forth across the congregation.

Some ministries seem to act carelessly with the funds that God has already brought into their hands for television ministry and spend a great proportion of their time trying to bring in even more money, usually with gimmicks or by big-name ministers visiting the set, instead of leveraging what they already have to bring in a greater harvest of souls to the Kingdom and depending on the unseen hand of God to supply more resources. If God is behind the program or project, His unseen hand will work on your behalf, and your *results (fruit)* will draw people to what you're doing. His anointing will break every yoke whenever the work at hand is called of Him.

Too many things being said, done, joked about, and sold from the pulpit and in front of cameras are born of the flesh, not of the Spirit. That's why they don't bear righteous fruit, and people have to be pressured to financially support the work. Righteous fruit from inspired, anointed works will always beat out gimmicks and exaggerated endorsements from the stage. I yearn for men and women of integrity and with God's anointing upon them to stand up and boldly proclaim His Word without falling into the trap of looking directly *to man* for provision to achieve their God-given callings.

Some men and women of God are participating in and earning large sums of money for motivational speaking (not ministry) and life coaching outside of religious organizations, using their name recognition as ministers alongside other "successful," secular, wealthy businessmen as a draw. We now have "mentors" abounding when we need righteous *disciplers* of men! Is it too time-consuming to disciple people in the ways of God, or do the spiritual hands get dirty down in the ditches with common people where they live?

Many ministers are writing books that are spiritually blank—they contain nothing life-giving between the pages, just stories and experiences and motivations that sell with enough heavy promotion. Some even get their staff members to consolidate a series of their sermons into a "new book" and claim to have written it themselves.

There are now ministers spending valuable time writing fiction books! That implies that people have read, studied, and fed on the Word of Truth enough; have spent enough time in prayer and intercession; and have done *enough* good fruit-bearing works so as to have time to read make-believe.

Good stewardship can be hard to discern at times because of the size or complexity of issues involved in today's churches. Some ministries are charging money for the use of "their" church for Christian events and concerts. Many traveling ministers are not allowing the taping of their messages at local churches where they speak, requiring that people purchase the CD or DVD from their own ministry organizations and not from the local church where their message was given. There are contracts, fees, secret agreements, or financial requirements mandated by some ministers before they will even come to your church or speak at your conference.

Is this stewardship of gifts or who has the biggest draw? Are we rock stars or ministers of the living God? Could up-front demands (special foods, transportation, minimum paycheck required, round-the-clock attendants, and so forth) like rock stars and other celebrities issue be a form of spiritual extortion? Is the desired goal of ministry deeper and deeper supernatural moves of the Spirit of God over people's lives, or is it flying home with a bigger and bigger paycheck in the breast pocket of the designer suit?

Gifts and possessions are for the Master's use in building His temple and receiving true worship, not for individuals to accumulate wealth or fame. Wealth and fame do not heal the sick or cast out evil spirits, nor have they ever operated in signs and wonders following the preaching of God's Word!

We must look back for a moment on some early Scriptural laws, statutes, ordinances, and commandments that God gave to His young nation, His people Israel. Exodus 23:8 says *to the ranks of leadership* in His new called-out nation, "And thou shalt take no gift: for the gift blindeth the wise, and perverteth the words of the righteous." Unfortunately, many ministers today *expect* or demand to be "blessed" with gifts for doing what is, essentially, their God-called duty to do: teach, preach, visit the sick, bless in marriage, counsel the troubled or broken, and other such things. The workman is certainly worthy of his hire but it is the responsibility of the people on the receiving end of ministry to offer the appropriate gift, given as a priestly offering and given with a willing heart.

Gifts of money, perks of privilege (chauffeured limousines, first-class tickets regardless of distance traveled, exclusive club memberships), and other entitlements have perverted the charismatic ministry in many places. Leaders were never to barter or sell their power, anointing, influence, or position for the sake of gain. Have some ministers and traveling singers found easy money from naïve or desperate sheep by using God's blessing (gifts, talent, anointing) for profit? There will come a day of reckoning for anyone guilty of shearing the sheep instead of feeding them.

Stewardship of ministry gifts demands a selfless heart for serving the people! We are not called to be merely life coaches, prosperity teachers, and success motivators running around speaking within privileged circles. We are to be *life-changers* for Christ: healers, disciplers of men, men under authority exercising God-given authority over oppressive demon spirits, stewards of resources building the Kingdom, and people of integrity who lead the lost out of darkness through the power of Christ.

Concerning stewardship of spiritual gifts and anointings, how many church services these days allow for the Holy Spirit to even operate in the gifts of the Spirit within the local body of believers? When did you last stand in a line in church for prayer for the sick and crippled? For deliverance for the oppressed?

How many born-again Christians are quickly channeled into a discipleship program to be loved and taught who they are in Christ, how to get started in Bible reading, how to recognize and deal victoriously with temptation, how to walk uprightly, how to be led by the Spirit, and how to get planted in the local church? Handing new converts a booklet or tape series does not qualify as discipleship and does not absolve ministries of their responsibility for discipling young Christians.

The fruits of modern church ministry are often hard to see because they are usually withered on the vine, anemic, needing a fresh infusion of love and power by the Holy Spirit to set free from all the encumbrances and sins that so easily entangle us (Heb. 12:1) and to provide a fresh anointing upon those in ministry whose faces are actively seeking God on bended knee.

Some ministers appear to have made themselves specialists in certain high-interest areas of Biblical studies: endtime events, the book of Revelation, Jewish feasts, miracles, Solomon's temple, the Ark of the Covenant, the Battle of Armageddon, and others. Does this specialty ministry draw a larger crowd? Does such focused teaching cater to "itching ears" in the Body and result in larger offerings and generate excitement independent of the move of the Spirit of God? Have such ministers lost sight of the calling, the privilege, and the heavy responsibility of *balanced ministry* inherent in their office gift to the Body of Christ? We need revolutionaries, radical men and women of faith who are God-pleasers and who are interested in building not their own Kingdoms, but the Father's Kingdom on Earth through faithful stewardship!

In a similar vein, there are gospel singers who have diluted or masked the clear message of Jesus, salvation, the blood, and Heaven so as to allow their music to cross over into secular markets, thus increasing the sales of their CD's manyfold. Their stage presence, dress, and actions do not seem to be focused as much on leading the people into a high level of worship in God's presence as it seems on giving a performance of their musical instruments and vocal abilities.

They produce CDs with bland lyrics devoid of anointing, with high-tech soundtracks and appealing secular riffs on the electric guitars. Worship leaders participate in synchronized head-banging and stutter-stepping around the stage, stiff-legged, just like rock stars in fleshly frenzies. Is God receiving this type of "praise and worship" as sweet incense in His nostrils, or has He already left the house? (God desires worship in the spirit of man toward Him. If you get your spirit-man truly worshipping, your soul and body must join in the praise and elevated adoration of the King of Glory.)

Some prominent gospel artists have quickly jumped to a more profitable secular music genre once they received enough exposure through their gospel recordings to flee the fold. Keep in mind that musical gifts and talents are given by God for His glory and will be judged together with ministry gifts, offices, administrations, and other gifts and talents.

How are these resources being used for the Master's building of His Body in your church? Is there consistent spiritual fruit being produced from the various ministries— healing of the sick, healing of broken marriages, reconciliation of parents with their children, restoration of repentant backsliders, and salvation of the lost? Does worship elevate the people's spirits toward God, collectively, and lead to His pleasure and adoration with the worship leader's help, or does it focus on specific human talents and essentially represent a performance that demands applause at the end of each song and feeds big egos? When judgment comes, it will start in His Church, beginning in the pulpit, then the stage areas, then moving to the pews. See 1 Peter 4:17: "For the time is come that judgment must begin at the house of God: and if it first begin at us, what shall the end be of them that obey not the gospel of God?"

I would like to clarify that I sincerely believe God blesses His people. It is His pleasure to bless and to prosper His own, even with great wealth. Scripture is full of examples of individuals who were truly blessed by a wide variety of means: through ungodly rulers; through ungodly nations; with land; with jewels and other riches; with animals; with gifts of the Spirit; with anointings; and with signs, wonders, and miracles. It is the popular message of prosperity that I feel is off base to a great extent and in sharp contrast to examples and principles of Biblical prosperity.

God's prosperity for His people is independent of the stock market and the health of any other economic benchmark. God's prosperity is contingent upon His spiritual blessings from above and favor being granted among men on Earth, whether in gaining authority, gaining recognition or fame from exploits that exalt God, receiving privileges, having access to power, or other difficult-to-achieve favors by those in authority. Often these favors result in material and financial blessing, but that is not a consistent result throughout Scripture.

Let's look at what God said about the subject in the 112th chapter of Psalms, which is in the center of a series of praise chapters spoken unto God by David in adoration and worship. I will summarize the *qualities* of a man that are recognized by God that entitle him to receive much blessing in various forms from God's hand. Some *results* of God's recognition of these qualities are also listed.

- He fears the Lord (judgments).
- He delights greatly in God's commandments.
- His progeny will be great upon the Earth.
- Being upright, he will be blessed.
- Wealth and riches shall be in his house.
- His righteousness endures (through the fruit of his works and through his seed).
- He receives God's light in the midst of darkness.
- He is gracious, full of compassion, and righteous.
- He is touched by people and lends.
- He is a man of discretion.
- He shall not be moved; his righteousness will always be remembered.
- He does not entertain fear because his heart is set on things above; he trusts God.
- He is not afraid of his enemies, for he leaves it to God to deal with them.
- He gives much and gives widely; he recognizes the needs of the poor.
- His life reflects enduring righteousness, and he will be exalted with honor.

For those who attain this degree of dedication to God and whose attitudes, motives, and desires are in alignment with these qualities, I can see why God will bless them abundantly with both spiritual and material riches. They will be givers, examples of maturity, lenders, and faithful stewards of all resources placed in their hands. They are spending time before God on their knees, seeking His direction in decisions, dying daily to themselves and their carnal desires, walking in humility, contributing greatly to the building of the Kingdom, and discipling others in holiness before God.

Perhaps such early and continuous indoctrination of kids by secularism in our hedonistic, modern society does not allow many

Christians to reach this level of maturity where they can be blessed with great wealth and monetary riches from God's hand and be unchanged by it. I desire to know men like David described, yet I have to read about them in the Bible.

I know from looking at the qualifications listed in this 112th chapter of Psalms that Jesus' words are so true that He spoke in the Gospel of Mark. A wealthy man came running up to Jesus, inquiring about how to secure eternal life. This man had diligently observed the Mosaic Law from childhood (good discipleship) and had great material wealth. Jesus loved him and wanted to help him obtain eternal life, so He told him the one thing that was lacking in the man's life: unwillingness to separate himself from his riches. His affections were too much set upon those possessions to take up his cross and follow Jesus.

> One thing thou lackest: go thy way, *sell whatsoever thou hast, and give to the poor,* and *thou shalt have treasure in Heaven:* and come, take up the cross, and follow me. And *he was sad* at that saying, and *went away grieved: for he had great possessions.* And Jesus looked round about, and saith unto his disciples, *How hardly shall they that have riches enter into the Kingdom of God!* And the disciples were astonished at his words. But Jesus answereth again, and saith unto them, Children, *how hard is it for them that trust in riches to enter into the Kingdom of God!* It is easier for a camel to go through the eye of a needle, than for a rich man to enter into the Kingdom of God.
>
> Mark 10:17–25, emphasis added

I have heard many attempts from pulpits at reducing the impact of Jesus' words and diluting their meaning in these Scriptures (sermons about how camels were loaded, gates were constructed into cities' market areas, merchants could pass through with only so much in goods, and so forth.). Do not be deceived by someone's attempt to justify wealth, love of money, or desire for greater material possessions by making it sound like Jesus said it was okay or that His lifestyle reflected wealth. I think His words are clear, direct, and reinforced consistently through the Gospels: your attitude toward your wealth and toward the poor are the essential baselines for self-examination.

The vast majority of wealthy men, Christian or not, do not meet those basic conditions touched on here in Mark's Gospel by Jesus or meet the qualifications listed above in Psalms. God wants faithful stewardship in this life and our eyes and affections set on things above; our real treasures will be waiting for us in Heaven.

Paul wrote to the Philippians and in the end of the letter made two very important points that should be learned: "Not that I speak in respect to want: for I have learned, in whatsoever state I am, therewith to be content.... But my God shall supply all your need according to his riches in glory by Christ Jesus" (Phil. 4:11, 19).

Paul did not encourage the Philippians to build up material possessions. He did not try to persuade them to reach and obtain a higher standard of living, let alone one of luxury. He did not even refer to the fulfilling of their needs through *material* items, but fulfilled according to *spiritual* resources that Jesus manages in Heaven. That excludes currencies, precious metals, automobiles, clothes, and all other *physical* manifestations. It includes spiritual blessings: gifts, operations, anointings, powers, supernatural talents, signs, and wonders.

Sometimes with faithful servants who are proven to be *faithful* stewards already *in small things,* God will bring great material resources into their hands. But it is always for the building of His Kingdom and for His glory. I'll focus my comments for now on the physical possessions that one may acquire under Biblical principles and how I think God blesses and prospers His people. I want to be rich in God and be under His blessing, regardless of what economic state I live within in this Earthly life.

If you study the lives of Abraham, Jacob, Noah, David, Solomon, Job, and the brief mention of others' material lives in the New Testament (even Ananias and Sapphira), you will see that however they obtained their wealth, whether through gifts, spoils of war, inheritance, or having God multiply their possessions (mostly animals), He required of them obedience and sacrifice that was *at a higher level* than the common people. He put much into their hands and expected much from them in return, whether in sacrificial giving from the heart or in obedience to God's command or to their own verbal commitment to God and His Church. (This is where Ananias and Sapphira erred terminally by being greedy and lying. Their penalty was sudden death.)

God blessed Abraham abundantly (Gen. 13:2) by giving him great riches from Pharaoh's own hand in Egypt; by giving him the possessions of some of his enemies in Canaan; by the hand of Abimelech, king of Gerar (Gen. 20); and by supernatural, abundant multiplication of his animals and his progeny (Exod. 23:26). In the same manner, God plundered more of Egypt's great wealth in later years to bless Joseph and then the nation of Israel at the exodus from Egypt (Exod. 3:21–22).

Read the passage of Scripture in Exodus 11:3 to see how God granted favor to Moses of all the people of Israel and Egypt, even Pharaoh's servants, *before* the Hebrew nation was finally told to leave. The Hebrews were able to begin collecting gold, silver, and jewels from their Egyptian neighbors right up until the time of actual departure.

Did you ever wonder where most of the gold, silver, and jewels for David's tabernacle and Solomon's temple came from? How ironic that God took from the existing world power (Egypt) and provided for His Hebrew people's economic needs and later for crafting anointed spiritual articles for His temple's sacrifices and worship. In each era of abundant wealth accumulation by God's people, it was for the purpose of building His tabernacle, His temple, or His Body of believers for His glory on Earth. Here are some self-directed questions that I have gleaned from examples in Scripture that guide me in how to make decisions about material possessions. Perhaps they will guide you, as well.

• Does the money or item have any particular attraction or fascination to me? If I can *freely give* it away at any time as God's Spirit directs or sell it to invest the proceeds into the Kingdom, then I have not set my affections on the item.

• Do I desire _____ (fill in the blank) more than I desire to hear God's voice or walk (minister) in a higher level of anointing? Some believers would rather have the perks of worldly success than to grow more deeply with God. Yes, shiny new luxury cars and large, modern estate homes are attractive to the soul, but they are merely wood, hay, and stubble in an eternal perspective. If we realize that fact, let's act like it and be about our Father's business while on Earth.

• What are my sources of pride: a big library of books, a four-car garage, my body's muscle tone, a country-club membership, a mountain home for summers, an extravagant set of special rims and tires, new golf clubs, a trophy wife, a baby grand piano in the special room I built for it, or the latest exotic kitchen upgrade and appliances? These will rust and become moth-eaten, with no eternal value except in how they can be used now to benefit the needy for the Kingdom of God—feeding the hungry, clothing the naked, providing shelter for the homeless, building orphanages and medical clinics, supplying the elderly and widows, and planting churches and missionaries throughout the dark recesses of this world.

Pride in possessions has to be transformed through the power of God into humility for service. Material possessions have to become God's property in our minds before we can be good stewards of them. If we try to satisfy our obligations to others without allowing our self-centeredness to die, we will be acting in a false humility before our Father, and our reward will be just.

• What do I think about and meditate on during my waking hours? I do want to be successful in *whatever God calls me to do*. Period. I want His blessing on those things that will enable me to fulfill His calling. I desire His gifts and anointings to work miracles in the lives of people I come into contact with during the day. I want His voice to speak out of my spirit each day, directing, correcting, comforting, strengthening, anointing, and emboldening me to do His will.

My success in those areas will determine my lifestyle, destination, perks, rewards, treasures, position of rulership, and fulfillment for all eternity. When I look back from Heaven, if I have been obedient to God in the stewardship of the things He placed in my hands, all other material issues will be considered fleeting and not of any consequence, except how they were used to increase my Father's Kingdom, His eternal house made of living stones.

- Is this possession in any way a hindrance to my testimony, to my life as an example to others, and to my ministry? Will it choke or diminish my anointing or give the wrong impression to others (by the possible appearance of evil)? Could it become a stumbling block to others? Does it hold me back in my desire to be a free giver?

  We may have possessions that are in excess of our needs or valued far more than we need. By selling them and adjusting our possessions to our actual needs, there will be money left over to sow into Kingdom outreach ministries and to allow God to have fruits of ministry to multiply.

- Do I look for new ways to make money? Are my goals, strategies, and tactics all Spirit-inspired and based on God's principles of stewardship and transparency before Him? What will I do with the *extra money* when I get it? Is it designated for me and my desires or for others less fortunate than I?

- Will my possessions in this Earthly life produce *an increase* for the Kingdom of God? If you can't answer yes, go back and read Jesus' parable of the talents given to the servants by the master.

- Do I tithe the minimum 10 percent of *gross* income and then give offerings freely beyond that? Some people will say,

"Wait a minute! I give 10 percent of my *net* income, and that's what I feel is acceptable as a tithe." If that is the way you think God established the tithe, then you will be judged as coming up short. God wants the *first* 10 percent of everything, not 10 percent of what is left over after federal taxes, state taxes, social security, health benefits co-payments, alimony, and 401K deductions have been removed. You, your family, and others can do as you please with the other 90 percent, but the *first* 10 percent goes to God as your tithe.

Look at Abraham, when he first tithed to Melchizedek of all his possessions (before there was currency) in Genesis 14:18–20. Melchizedek appeared in Scripture without a beginning or end and is a foreshadowing of Christ. Like Jesus, he simultaneously occupied the three anointed offices of prophet, priest, and king, probably in the same location as the future Jerusalem.

In Genesis 28:22, we see Jacob's response to God's powerful message of blessing and prosperity: "And of all that thou shalt give me I will surely give the tenth unto thee." He didn't say that he would give a tenth after animal food and servant expenses had been deducted or after his travel costs to Bethel had been reimbursed.

Malachi 3:8–12 in the New Living Translation gives an excellent snapshot of how God looks at the principles of tithing and giving.

> Should people cheat God? Yet you have cheated me! But you ask, "What do you mean? When did we ever cheat you?" You have cheated me of the tithes and offerings due to me. You are under a curse, for your whole nation has been cheating me. Bring all the tithes into the storehouse so there will be enough food in my Temple. If you do, says the Lord of Heaven's Armies, I will open the windows of Heaven for you. I will pour out a blessing so great you won't have enough room to take it in! Try it! Put me to the test! Your crops will be abundant, for I will guard them

from insects and disease. Your grapes will not fall from the vine before they are ripe, says the Lord of Heaven's Armies. Then all nations will call you blessed, for your land will be such a delight, says the Lord of Heaven's Armies.

Is God first or not in your life? Is the proportion of your giving like the widow who gave the mite, or instead, is it like the rich man's gift? Do you want to be blessed? Are you going to be obedient to God's law of provision for the body and its ministry? Let me encourage you to be generous with your assets, for they came to you by the hand of God for a temporal window of time for your use in building the Kingdom of God on Earth.

Unfortunately, in the Body of Christ, we have too many believers trying to look, act, dress, party, play, talk, work, and make financial decisions like those "successful" ones around them belonging to the world of darkness. The lines separating the two groups have blurred, and the monetary value systems are essentially the same. We need to get on our knees and seek holiness, righteousness, transparency, and humility before God for Him to transform our desires for the temporal to fervent desires for the eternal!

Faithful stewardship is based on the condition of the heart toward pleasing God. It is incumbent upon Christians to set themselves apart from material lusts for the Master's use and to do the works that Jesus did. Proverbs 28 is a good chapter to examine regarding how God views all these issues of materialism, riches, prosperity, blessings, and motives.

1. Verse 8: "He that by usury and unjust gain increaseth his substance, he shall gather it for him that will pity the poor."

Oops! That says if you make your fortune by charging interest and taking advantage of people unjustly, your fortune may be given to someone whose heart is right toward the needy and poor. I see a lot of businesses flourishing that cater to the poor and charge ridiculously high interest rates for short-term loans, advances on paychecks, car titles, mortgages, and other possessions. The ones in need often cannot repay the amount with burdensome interest on time and then lose their cars or homes, which may result in their losing their jobs. These business people will be accountable to God for their dealings with the poor.

2. Verse 10: "But the upright shall have good things in possession."

    Things that are good for you to possess may not be in the form of jewels, luxury cars, and fur coats.

3. Verse 11: "The rich man is wise in his own conceit."

    Rich men are easily deluded, believing lies interjected from the pit because of their growing pride in possessions and their independence from other people.

4. Verse 16: "But he that hateth covetousness shall prolong his days."

    The righteous are obedient already to God's commandment about not coveting what other people (the Joneses) have obtained.

5. Verses 20–22: "A faithful man shall abound with blessings: but he that maketh haste to be rich shall not be innocent. To have respect of persons is not good: for for a piece of bread that man will transgress. He that hasteth to be rich hath an evil eye, and considereth not that poverty shall come upon him."

    Are you faithful in your stewardship of what God has already placed within your hands? Are you looking for His blessing as the source of your prosperity, or instead, are you determined to make your fortune on your own by whatever means?

    Another point: It is common for a man whose wealth is rising to become more sensitive (and deferential) to those who can help him, as opposed to those who need him and his help. This is blatant respect of persons, or partiality, currying favor with a select few who can provide something key to moving up the next rung on the ladder of success. Usually, when this attitude sets in, the poor and those who cannot further the ascent into greater success are ignored, since they are now considered unneeded. This is conceit, arrogance, self-importance, and respect of persons.

Do you long to be rich, thinking about it and setting goals to obtain wealth? Be careful, for that attractive road is full of potholes that arise from hell to steal, kill, and destroy its travelers.

6. Verse 28:"He that giveth unto the poor shall not lack: but he that hideth his eyes shall have many a curse."

We read earlier Jesus' story about the rich man who turned his eyes from the beggar at his gate. His fate was made very clear. Based on this Scripture's description of the reward of giving to the poor, you will have sufficiency merely by giving to the poor. Put that together with God's principles of multiplication for giving out of your heart of love and you have a formula for success in life. "Not lacking" and "achieving sufficiency" do not translate into having a new Ferrari sitting in the driveway or a Gucci watch on the wrist.

Where is your treasure? This need to serve our Master will direct our desires toward stewardship and service through good works. That necessitates the use of various forms of the world's currency and material possessions to achieve God's purposes. He will place those resources into yielded hands with clean hearts. Those will be the *prosperous* people in His Kingdom on Earth.

First Corinthians 4:2 says, "Moreover it is required in stewards, that a man be found faithful." I doubt that we or the general public will see or hear much from these truly prosperous believers because God will be doing great works through them out *among the people,* as Jesus did in His ministry.

God wants us to do His work without fanfare, without headlines or cameras, and in private so we do not end up receiving credit or glory for the results. Secular philanthropists know these principles well: give away your resources, but make the legal and financial arrangements in private in order to avoid exposure and recognition that could hinder or abort projects.

We must be about our Father's business (will) of building His Kingdom and bringing Him glory with everything He gives to us, without concern for ourselves! It is to God's glory, not to the fame and wealth of individuals who prominently display their names in lights over everything done in the name of God.

Let's take an interesting trip into Ezekiel and see a few things that led to the downfall of Satan, when he was known as Lucifer in Heaven. These issues are the same as the principles that I have discussed already that lead mankind to fail as faithful stewards.

Ezekiel 28:2 addresses the spiritual strongman, the prince and real king over Tyrus (coastal Tyre in modern Lebanon), Satan himself. A few of the early references are probably directed to Satan's stooge, the human king of Tyrus, but it is clear where Satan is specifically described: "in your great pride" (NLT). Here we have the foundational root problem exposed—the sin of pride. Let's see what things led to pride (all verses in the New Living Translation).

Verse 4: "With your wisdom and understanding you have *amassed great wealth—gold and silver* for your treasuries" (emphasis added).

Verse 5: "Yes, your wisdom has made you *very rich,* and your riches have made you *very proud"* (emphasis added).

Verse 12: "You were the *model of perfection,* full of wisdom and *exquisite in beauty"* (emphasis added).

Verse 13: "You were in Eden, the garden of God. Your *clothing was adorned* with every precious stone—[I will not list them here]—all *beautifully crafted for you* and set in the finest gold. They were given to you on the day you were created" (emphasis added).

Verse 14: "I ordained and anointed you as the *mighty* angelic guardian" (emphasis added).

Verse 16: "Your *rich commerce* led you to violence, and you sinned" (emphasis added).

Verse 17: "Your heart was filled with pride *because of all your beauty.* Your wisdom was *corrupted by your love of splendor"* (emphasis added).

Verse 18: "You defiled your sanctuaries with your many sins and your *dishonest trade*_(emphasis added).

How close to home do some of these words come: love of great wealth, riches, pride, beauty, splendor, rich commerce, adorned with luxurious clothing, being a model of perfection, exquisite in beauty, and dishonest trade? Do any of them fit your lifestyle or ministry? Are these things that you seek?

These are in stark contrast to models of humility, modesty, and holiness. For example, the latest secular clothing fashions should not become prevalent in the Body of Christ, for they are based upon worldly motives and worldly appeals—sensual, erotic, or self-aggrandizing; reflecting prison garb; or allied with other forms of ungodliness, such as laziness/slouchiness, indifference, and rebellion. Christians must "come out" from the world. We can be casual or well dressed without looking, sounding, and acting like the world of darkness outside the church.

First Peter 2:9 summarizes well the privilege and the responsibility we must both acknowledge and walk in: "But ye are a chosen generation, a royal priesthood, *an holy nation,* a *peculiar people;* that ye should shew forth the praises of him who hath called you *out of darkness* into his marvelous light" (emphasis added). Within the Body of Christ, we should not look, sound, walk, or act like Hollywood starlets or thugs on the street corner.

In Ephesians 5:27, Paul is talking about the Church of Jesus Christ and His acceptance of the Body: "That he might present it to himself a glorious church, not having spot, or wrinkle, or any such thing; but that *it should be holy* and without blemish" (emphasis added). The style and degree of dress are not as important as are the attitudes, the motives, and the desires behind them. Let us seek holiness before God in our prayer closets and die to fashion trends, music trends, sports trends, and what is currently "cool" in the world. It is God whom we should seek to please with all of our hearts and available resources. Whatever happened to believers' acquiring of a sense of holiness, of modesty, and of selfless humility when changed by the awesome power of God's love and forgiveness? This is a spiritual issue that we all have to confront in order to walk before God and our fellow man in a manner that reflects our inward spirit.

From the clothing-fashion example above, it is not an issue as much about the clothes and overall appearance as it is the attitude, the motive, the pride, the carriage of the person, and the person's influence on others in the Body, particularly youth. In most cases, pastors and teachers are not giving instruction on and discipling people in true holiness, an attitude and lifestyle both internal toward God (spirit-man) and external to the world (both of the soul and flesh). People are being left to reach their own conclusions about standards of holiness, and most of them are not yet anchored in the Word of Truth or diligent about prayer and fasting. They see the popular music, dress styles, jewelry, body art, surgical enhancements, and so forth of the world system and bring that culture right into the church.

We don't look or sound much like a separated people anymore. We are seeing much carnal fruit today from an unbalanced emphasis in teaching and preaching on prosperity, a distorted view of Christian success, an exaggerated feel-good method of motivating people, and hardly any discipleship or teaching on service, dying to self daily, holiness before God and man, and submission to those in authority (whether spiritual, secular, or governmental). We believers cannot be faithful stewards without being spiritually whole, balanced in the Word, fitting together well in love, and bringing glory to our Father by our works.

Regardless of the source of the possessions—from inheritance, from offerings, from earned trade or job income, from gifts from others—we must pay tithes on them to the local church body, give generously to others, support outreach ministries and evangelistic missions, and then release what's left of them to God for His use as He directs a compliant, submissive heart. Remember how hard it is for a rich man to enter Heaven (as Jesus taught), but every man entering Heaven will become instantly rich beyond anything he has ever imagined or could ever receive as an estimated value!

Some rich people will enter Heaven; as we know, Abraham, Isaac, and Jacob did. They were *abundantly* blessed by God in material possessions. Abraham was *God's friend,* instantly obedient, who loved and welcomed strangers, was an intercessor, had pure motives, and was faithful. God prospered him greatly so that Abraham always had *available resources* for whatever opportunity or need arose. For example, when his brother died, Abraham was able to adopt his nephew Lot into his family without any resource limitation and provide Lot with the discipleship and upbringing that made him a man of God.

Abraham could be trusted to be a wise and faithful steward, never afraid of losing what he had because he knew it belonged to God (even his only son of old age). He could function in whatever God asked of him without the financial pressures and limited resources that other less blessed, less prosperous men and women of God face. Did Moses (or Joseph or David or Solomon) ever seem to let all the gold and abundant wealth under his authority affect his judgment, his motives, or his goals? Are you that kind of steward?

Jesus' walk on Earth should be our primary example of stewardship. He had such a relationship with the Father that His followers shared all things. He never had a house of His own, his own bed, a stock of animals, or new and different changes of fine clothing hanging in a closet. He never planned where His next meal was going to be. People were changed in their hearts when they saw and heard Him, and they gave Him everything He needed.

People loved Him and His ministry to them, a selfless service and powerful love that produced abundant, consistent fruit. His presence and the fruits of His ministry compelled them to serve Him to such an extent that all His needs were met during His continual travels around Israel. The disciples and apostles experienced the same result of ministry. Look at the Scriptures where Jesus told them not to worry about those things, because they would be supplied to them.

I'm certain that many thousands of people gave money and possessions to Jesus and His men because of His news of salvation and the great healings that occurred in their midst. Jesus even designated one of the disciples to be His treasurer to receive money and goods, make accounting for them, and distribute for their needs and the people around them. However, I know from reading His own words the principles that guided Jesus in handling His Father's possessions as a faithful steward: He gave back to the needy, obeyed Scripture and paid His tithes, and gave large offerings. He kept nothing back for Himself.

Jesus taught stewardship to those around Him *by example,* just as He taught serving, healing and deliverance through His name, submission to God's will, Kingdom authority, and other key principles of living and working for the Kingdom. He was on a mission, and He has commissioned us with the same directive: build the Kingdom of God across the Earth, with living stones, with resources placed under our stewardship, upon the foundation set by God, and upon the Chief Cornerstone that is firmly in place.

The New Testament Church had zeal for their salvation and for the care of others in their communities, feelings that had been rare to see before and that have been rare to see since. However, they had just witnessed the works of the Son of God and had heard His teaching. They learned firsthand from Jesus how to be prosperous and bless others through generosity and other acts of love.

Acts 4:34 gives one clear example of the members acting for the good of the community as Jesus had taught. In the New Living Translation, it reads, "There were *no needy people* among them, because those who owned land or houses would sell them and bring the money to the apostles to give to those in need" (emphasis added). We aren't told if this describes the liquidation of their own personal residence and property or if it refers to additional houses and land that they owned, similar to today's rental properties, second homes at the beach or in the mountains, investment real estate, time-share condominiums, or similar possessions.

What we do see here is the commitment to use their own personal possessions to build the Kingdom of God, spreading the gospel and meeting the needs of their fellow believers. There were some, like Ananias and Sapphira, who were greedy and secretly held back money that they had committed to the local church. They paid a high price for reneging on their vow to God.

God wants to touch our hearts and get us away from storing up vast retirement packages (far in excess of what we need), building bigger and nicer homes, buying more expensive cars, and leading a truly consumer lifestyle. He wants His people to become givers, producers, sharers, lenders, suppliers, donors, and philanthropists who do not place great importance on material possessions, understanding their place and their value in building His Kingdom and recognizing the accountability to which each will be held one day soon. That is Biblical stewardship.

Being Spirit-Led Versus Opportunity or Compulsion

Are there many issues in our walk with God more important than being Spirit-led? Every day on Earth, we have decisions to make: which school to attend, which job to take, which mate to choose, how to prepare the best speech, what to write, or whether to testify about something or to keep it solely in prayer. We wonder, *Is God directing me to pray with that person? Who is the best choice for that job? Should I go there? When is the ideal time to tell him? What should I do with that spiritual dream I had last night? Should I commit to this church? Why am I feeling a compulsion to take the other direction home today?* These questions and many others are daily thoughts that we all face, and we live our lives from moment to moment making an almost continuous stream of decisions that determine our happiness, our safety, our success, our financial strength, and all the other qualities that we call "who I am" in this world.

As critical as each decision point potentially could be in its long-term consequences, how does God play a role in those decisions for the believer? Do you stop what you're doing and pray about each one that arises throughout the day? Do you pray in the evening about all of them that you've saved up during the day, delaying the decisions until later? The answer to these, for me, is no. I can see no examples of this type of behavior in either the Old or New Testaments.

Unfortunately, some people tend to allow pressures and people—not God—to influence their decisions. These same people may be so accustomed to their circumstances and feelings coercing their decisions that they cannot relate to receiving spiritual guidance. They are unable to see whether they are being persuaded to make a decision by an opportunity opening for them or by being driven by a compulsion. Let me say at this very point that the majority of what we call compulsions are demon-driven carnal desires— for success, for recognition, for drugs, for food, for alcohol/caffeine/nicotine, for wealth, for acceptance, or for some other means of gratification.

This makes it vitally important to know the will of God and to let Him lead us by His Spirit. We need to know when a true opportunity has been opened *by Him* and also be able to recognize unrighteous compulsions when they arise in us. If we can sort out the chaff from the wheat in our Christian walk, we will be led to make the right decisions and avoid the pain of poor choices outside of God's plan for us.

Jesus said in John 10:27 in the New Living Translation, "My sheep *listen to my voice;* I know them, and they follow me" (emphasis added). We have to *want* to hear His voice and get ourselves positioned to hear it through whatever channel He chooses to communicate with us.

I hope this chapter will open up some new insights for you in knowing how to make decisions based on your relationship with God and how He chooses to lead you from one day to the next. Remember, the assumption I am making in this subject matter is that you love God with all your heart, have made Him Lord of your life (after accepting Him as Savior), are feeding upon His living Word regularly, and praying regularly. Otherwise, you will not be able to fully benefit from this instruction on being Spirit-led. I would also hope that you have sought to be filled with His Spirit and that the Holy Spirit is giving your human spirit *ears to hear* from God.

Let's first explore some of the various ways that God has led His people through the written history of His relationship to His chosen people.

1. In the Garden of Eden, Adam *walked and talked* daily with God, particularly in the cool of the day (Gen. 3:8–9). We do not know what form or covering God took for this intimate relationship and communication. God spoke directly and audibly to Adam, as He did with others such as Moses, Noah, and Jesus. What a privilege for Adam to have direct access to God and walk with Him and talk with Him in the garden, up until sin entered his spirit!

   Adam had been created in purity of spirit, soul, and body, and there had been no sin to limit his relationship with God or his capacity to encounter God in His unknown (to us) form of glory in the garden. God had made him "the god of Earth" for rulership and thought of Adam as His chosen one of creation, His peculiar treasure, the firstborn of many to worship and adore their Heavenly Father on Earth as the angels did in Heaven. God communed directly with his beautiful creation made in His image. I am confident that He was a proud Father!

   Unfortunately, this blessed duo of God's creation in the garden tripped up before hardly getting started because of their poor exercise of free will, one of the unique God-given qualities of mankind. After the sin episode, Adam only heard the voice of God moving through the garden, letting him know of the presence of God. Adam's original purity had been contaminated with sin, and its toxic effects brought in fear, embarrassment, shame, and deceitfulness. God could not be in the presence of sin, and Adam disqualified himself and all mankind from knowing God in the fullness of relationship, which I feel Adam had been privileged to enjoy for a season.

   You may recall that God would have shown Himself to Moses many years later when Moses asked to see His glory, but He knew that Moses could not have survived such an encounter because of the inherent sin of Adam. Instead, God had Moses stand in a cleft of rock to limit his exposure by partially shielding him from the awesome (and deadly to humans with sin) glory of His face while God passed quickly by him. For Moses' added safety, God placed His hand over Moses to block His face and allowed Moses a glimpse of His back parts (Exod. 33:18–23) as

He walked past him. Later, in Numbers 12:8, we read how God points out to Miriam and Aaron (who were being called before Him for their presumption) that He spoke "mouth to mouth" with Moses, He spoke directly and clearly to Moses about the content of His subjects, and He presented Himself to Moses in a form that Moses could live and not die. The encounters with merely a representation of God were so awesome that they made the skin of Moses' face to shine afterward.

2. God spoke directly out of Heaven, in or through a cloud, a cloud pillar, a mist, or a pillar of fire to His *chosen people* in many Scriptures. Read the life of Moses and Jesus for several nice examples of God's speaking to *a group of believers*. Exodus 19:9–25 and 20:18–22 relate details of God's choosing to appear in a thick cloud before the nation of Hebrews on Mount Horeb (Sinai). He had to dwell within the thick cloud while He spoke to the people so that His brightness/holiness/glory would not be beheld by Adamic sin in the people and cause their death.

   Even with His presence essentially filtered by the thick cloud, read what an awesome atmosphere the people found themselves close to: thunder and lightning, a thick cloud upon the mountain, the already loud voice of a trumpet getting louder and louder, the entire mountain appearing to smoke like a furnace because of the fire of God, and the entire mountain quaking as in an earthquake. The people trembled and wanted no more words or appearance from God. I believe that this is the *least common* method of communication from God to man, based on Bible study and on following the movements of God in the twentieth- and twenty-first-century Church.

   One powerful image of the visible pillar of fire of God (going before and hovering over the people after their exodus from Egypt) that I love to meditate upon is a vision in my mind of the children of Israel encamped in a plain or in the desert as they slowly made progress during forty challenging years to reach Canaan. In the center of the encampment is the tabernacle containing the Ark of the Covenant, which held the tablets of the laws of God. Arising from the tabernacle is an enormous pillar of fire spreading out over the camp and lighting the entire area, providing constant awareness of His presence over and among His people.

If you were part of a heathen tribe of Canaanites approaching this encampment to attack it at sunrise and plunder its wealth, wouldn't you have been shocked to see this sight as you crept up a hillside to look down upon the camp? Yes, you would have wondered on the way up why it wasn't dark during the night on the other side of the hill, thinking that a full moon must be out. At the moment you saw the display of the fire of God over His people, I think you and all your fellow warriors would have sunk to the ground, at first frozen in terror and then shaking with fear at that sight. All thoughts of attack would have drained from your mind as quickly as your weapons fell to the ground! That is why Rahab for years had heard the men of the wicked city speak with great fear about the children of Israel's God going before them into the land. I'm sure that they heard the description of that scene from other neighboring nations as well as from their own scouts.

The Bible tells us that God was also *walking throughout* the Israeli encampment of people, not just hovering above them (see 2 Sam. 7:6–7; Deut. 23:14.) It was out of the cloud and the pillar of fire that He spoke (or tried to speak) to Israel. They were so carnal-minded that they feared hearing His voice and wanted Him to speak through Moses to them. Eventually, only two of this original stiff-necked group from Egypt made it into Canaan: Joshua and Caleb.

I see a correlation; the closer the people were to God (loving and obeying Him), *the clearer they heard His voice* and the less fear they felt. Some examples we're given in Scripture show the people recoiling in terror at His voice; others describe the people hearing a muffled sound, like thunder, in the distance. That still holds true today.

In contrast to that, look at Abraham, the friend of God, and his relationship and communications with God. Elijah, too, heard clearly God's instructions. So did Elisha and David, among others *who loved and obeyed* God. You will be able to hear God's voice speaking to you more clearly as you spend more time loving and obeying Him—praying, feeding upon His living Word, acting on your faith through works, building His Body, meditating upon His Word, and praising and worshipping Him throughout the day. What do you hear, and how clear is it for making decisions?

3. God also spoke through the Urim and Thummim. These items are a mystery, for the most part, but Scripture does reveal some aspects of them that show clearly that they were provided by God and were to be used for judging, for decision-making, and for direction. This process that God established for using the Urim and Thummim for a time is not revealed to us through Scripture but seems to have been another channel of communication from God to His people. God may have told Moses all about it and he informed the people, because the first mention of the Urim and Thummim in Exodus leaves the impression that the people already understood what they were and how they were to be used for direction by the high priest.

   I'm going to refer to these articles collectively as "them" in my discussion, as opposed to "it." They are usually not mentioned individually and seem to have a purpose best (or fully) met when acting together in unity as one single instrument of God. (Does that sound familiar?)

   When God was first establishing the formal priesthood and its articles of clothing and service, He instructed Moses about the general placement of the Urim and Thummim in the breastplate of judgment so that the Urim and Thummim might be upon the heart of the high priest when he went into the Holy of Holies. Try to imagine, when that perfect light shone through the twelve precious stones, what an awesome and beautiful sight it would have been! Perhaps the priest would still be able to tell of God's answer or direction with his eyes closed or in darkness because of the intensity of light generated and the warmth given off.

   I think it is noteworthy that this specific place to be located on the high priest is identified by God for supernatural direction. It was located precisely over the heart. Today we are the priesthood of believers, and we have direct access to God in prayer through the work of Jesus. As the nation of Israel was represented by twelve precious stones with a tribal name written on each, we today are the living stones of God's house, with His name written upon our foreheads! His perfect light shines out through each re-created human spirit and provides guidance. His Word (Jesus) is a lamp unto our feet and a light to our path, as the Urim and Thummim were to the high priest at that time. It is a beautiful set of parallels to think about.

These words, *Urim* and *Thummim,* would best be translated as "light" and "perfection," not in a single or general expression, but as in the ultimate, superlative use of each word. Of course, that definition would apply to anything from God by virtue of its purity and its completeness of function. Imagine light or lights in the fullest sense: the glory of God, or in the natural, the up-close visible light from a huge star in space. Although this is difficult for us to grasp, it may be easier to think of perfection personified: the Lamb of God, our High Priest, the majesty of God, Heaven's precious gemstones and metals that are transparent in their state of purity. Each is complete, perfect, pure, and exhibiting its fullness of purpose.

Read in Exodus 28:30, Numbers 27:21, Deuteronomy 33:8, 1 Samuel 28:6, Ezra 2:63, and Nehemiah 7:65 the references to the Urim and Thummim. They were essentially consulted for direction (perfect illumination), and the assumption is that they glowed brightly behind or as part of the twelve precious stones of the tribes of Israel fixed in four rows of three in the breastplate of judgment.

The Urim and Thummim were the high priest's only direct connection to God when he was not before Him in the Holy of Holies once each year. To my understanding of this form of godly communication, the high priest could inquire of God and receive an answer by the stones lighting up for a *yes.* He didn't have to call for Moses, the only judge/prophet of Israel at the time (that we know of), for answers within his areas of responsibility. My assumption, also, is that no light emanating from behind the precious stones by the question posed meant a *no.*

Should we go to war? Is this man guilty of lying? Have I offered sufficient burnt offerings for this iniquity? The high priest held an anointed office, and he had to know the mind of God to walk in absolute obedience. To make an error or an omission usually resulted in the death of the high priest. Later, when God had chosen and anointed multiple judges and prophets within Israel, it seems that the need for the Urim and Thummim for direction and decision-making through the high priest ended.

God had a better way to communicate throughout His growing Hebrew nation of believers. His instructions seem to have then been commonly voiced directly to each anointed judge/ prophet, high priest, and (later) king of His people. There was no further mention of the Urim and Thummim made regarding their presence or continued use within the priesthood. Read *Unger's Bible Dictionary* for additional insights into possibilities of the meaning and function of the Urim and Thummim.

4. At rare times God has spoken to *unbelievers* or through an *animal* (donkey). These are certainly exceptions to the typical methods of communication to man, and those examples involved imme- diate warning of impending destruction. He wrote on a banquet- room wall for a huge group of pagans. He allowed the spirit of Samuel to be called up by a witch in order to admonish King Saul a day before his death, to explain some hard things, and to date the impending death of Saul and his sons. Saul was out of relationship with God by then and was stooping to consult a witch at Endor for guidance. In this instance with this previously anointed king, the communication was *not direct* from God, because Saul had lost his anointing and done evil in the land.

5. The more common method of communication from God to man in the Old Testament Scriptures was for Him to speak directly to His *anointed servant,* whether prophet/prophetess, priest, or king. People outside of those anointed offices had little hope of ever hearing the voice of God, except for the few times He spoke openly to His assembled people.

He may have spoken audibly or in a small voice within the person. We usually aren't told enough detail about the communication to know exactly how the voice came: prophecy through inspiration, using the subject's own voice; providing inspiration to write down instructions; or God's instructions being written upon the mind of the person (Noah getting detailed instructions or drawings on how to build the ark; Moses on the mountain for weeks getting a massive download from Heaven on all the details of building the Ark of the Covenant, priestly garments, procedures and ordinances to adhere to, rites of sacrifice, feasts, acceptable behavior, righteous judgment, and the Sabbath laws; and Solomon getting massive quantities of detailed instruction on building the temple, its materials of construction, the contractors to use, architectural and metallurgical details, and so forth).

Many prophets stated in Scripture, "The word of the Lord came unto me." It could have been written across the sky above or appeared to him written in soil or sand at the prophet's feet. We don't know the various methods God used to speak to His chosen ones, even in those instructions of which we have a written record in His Word of Truth.

In New Testament days through today, we have no more anointed kings or priests to look to for direction. Fortunately, we are kings and priests of the Kingdom of God through the sacrifice of the Lamb of God for our sins, creating new sinless spirits within us that are able to commune directly with God. His Spirit of Truth lives within our spirits and gives inspiration, revelation, prophecy, tongues and interpretation of tongues, a word of knowledge, or a word of wisdom to us.

We do have prophets of God still in our midst, although they are not generally recognized by churches or ministries and could never win popularity contests because of the gravity of their ministry. I am not attempting in this book to cover the New Testament anointed ministry offices of the body, gifts of the Spirit, administrations, helps, or other related subjects. There have been many excellent books on these subjects by some profound writers that I would encourage you to obtain and study: the late Derek Prince, the late Kenneth E. Hagin, the late Gordon

Lindsey, Jack Hayford, the late Lester Sumrall, and others who have had a deep walk with God and many spiritual encounters with God. Study the Word, and read some books from these authors; then you will have a good working knowledge of God's operations and communications in today's Body.

6. One awesome form of communication used rarely has been through an appearance—in a burning bush, an angel, Jesus as the Angel of the Lord, Jesus as Himself, for example—with direct verbal messages to the *individuals.* In some cases, the one doing the appearing was in a natural, physical form that the human eye could see. Examples like this in Scriptures throughout the Bible include Abraham, Moses, Solomon, Paul, and Stephen.

    In other cases, the spiritual eyes of the believer were opened to see into the spirit realm. (This is the gift of the Spirit called *discerning of spirits,* often mistakenly called the gift of discernment. You can see into the spirit realm as the Holy Spirit operates that gift through you. You may see angels, other creatures of Heaven, saints of God, or various levels of demon spirits in that spirit dimension outside the physical dimension.) Look at 2 Kings 2:11–12, 2 Kings 6:17, and Luke 1:11–19 as examples of this marvelous gift in operation through yielded hearts.

7. As in the Old Testament Scriptures, God still communicates through dreams and visions. With visions, you may see clearly what is intended for you to see, with all the detail supplied. Or, you may experience what I call a minivision, a mere glimpse of what is now or is to come, with much less clarity and detail provided. Those dreams and visions are the *channels* through which the information flows, but it is the *message* that is important to understand. The message may be one of current events and relationships (a word of knowledge) or of future events and relationships (a word of wisdom).

    I'll give an example of a minivision that God gave to me years ago when we were in great need of a second car. Our two children were riding in the back of our only car, and my wife was with us; we were going home from some local event. As we approached a stoplight, I looked over to the right and across a sizeable commercial parking lot. Immediately my attention was drawn to the front row of cars in front of the buildings and focused upon the second car to the right.

Instantly I heard the voice of God's Spirit speak to me (through my spirit) clearly and say, "I'm going to give you that car." I turned and wondered what, if anything, to say to my wife. Some people other than Lee would have thought that I'd had too much sun in my face and had imagined the scene and the voice. But we both knew our Father's voice from other times of communication, and she listened to the details of the unexpected experience as we continued to drive home: the car my attention was diverted to was a later model, white, midsize, four-door General Motors sedan. I had no time to see any other details except the immediate impression given in the brief vision.

As with other previous dreams, visions, and messages from God, we kept this in our hearts and didn't share it with anyone, except God in prayer. Some six to eight months later, a couple from out of state called to say that they wanted to come visit us for the weekend and asked if it would be convenient. We welcomed them into our home, and they quickly got to the reason for their visit—they felt led to buy us a car!

To be honest, by this time I had forgotten the vision and the message. I had not been faithful to hold fast to God's word until seeing it fulfilled. Despite my forgetfulness, that night we had a two-year-old, low-mileage, white, four-door Oldsmobile Cutlass Ciera sedan sitting in the driveway, looking like a new one and looking exactly like the car shown to me in the vision months earlier.

When Lee saw it, she began to weep, for she remembered what I had described in the vision. God was faithful to perform His word in our life. When the reality of His provision hit me as she reminded me of His promise, I was speechless for several minutes and so thankful to my God for His supply.

In our lives, Lee is the dreamer and God shows her many things each week, some happening in people's lives now, some yet to come. For me, I have a few spiritual dreams and a few minivisions, the majority pertaining to future events. All these experiences that are truly spiritual require discussion about them with the Father, their source—praying or interceding for the people shown, asking for an interpretation of an abstract or unclear message, asking what to do or say or when to act on what has been shown.

Without God's direction, it is not wise to even talk about or act on these messages. Discretion, good judgment, and God's leading are required for effective (life-giving) results when acting on these types of messages. We may not have the right understanding of the situation, or it may not be the right time, God's time, to act.

8. The most common method in today's dispensation of grace for being led by God is through His Spirit leading us in our study of His Word. From the Word providing the principles, truths, and examples that we are to follow, it is our responsibility to *act* on those things that we learn.

His living Word of Truth was given to us for direction, as we would use a road map to get somewhere in the physical realm. In His Word (Jesus), He tells us His character and what pleases or displeases Him. Based solely on that instruction and the examples given, we have an answer to many of life's decisions, since we can choose to do what we know pleases God.

Conversely, we know that there are many things that He hates, that He abhors, or that are not good for our benefit. Following those rules, commandments, and the teachings of Jesus, we can decide what *not* to do. We also learn the principles of stewardship, of serving others, partaking of communion, of obedience, of honoring the Sabbath, of tithing and giving, of not becoming unequally yoked, of loving our enemies, and many other things. From this instruction, we are able to correctly make many other daily decisions in life.

Remember the verse that I referenced earlier in Psalm 119:105 about the light that God's Word brings before us for guidance? Look now at Psalm 1:2–3 in the New Living Translation. This is referring to *blessed* men: "But they delight in the law of the

Lord, meditating on it day and night. They are like trees planted along the riverbank, bearing fruit each season. Their leaves never wither, and they prosper in all they do."

Note that believers who feed upon the living Word will be delighted (thrilled) by it because of the life that issues forth and will consequently meditate (think) on it day and night. Is that you, or is your Bible study less interesting? Perhaps you are not hungering and thirsting for the Word (Jesus) sufficiently enough that it (He) is able to transform your mind (soul) and give direction as God speaks to you through it (Himself).

Furthermore, the psalm said that you will be like a sturdy tree along the riverbank and that you will bear fruit consistently in its season. As a tree, your leaves will never wither because your roots are drinking from the River of Life. The icing on the cake is the last point of this psalm: you will prosper in everything you do in life—education, marriage, parenting, church ministry, retirement, stewardship, job, and everything else.

The Bible is a critically valuable source of communication directly from God to you. Much of what you read or hear from it goes straight into your spirit, which is alive to God, whether your understanding grasps it all at the time or not. The Holy Spirit can and will turn it over inside you and bring enlightenment when you truly desire it!

9. The last form of communication with God that I will discuss is that of being *led by His Spirit* within your human spirit. In many Christians, unfortunately, this direct and live input from God is underdeveloped. Together with Bible knowledge, these channels are the most common ways for God to communicate His will to His Body members. God desires to speak to all His children but is hindered by many obstacles.

   a. Lack of desire by the individual to hear God's voice.
   b. Lack of knowledge of His Word (Bible study!).
   c. Lack of faith (or unbelief), which usually comes from lack of knowledge of His Word and not being planted in a local church body. Jesus tells us that unbelief stopped Him from

doing great works in His hometown of Nazareth: "And he did not many mighty works there because of their unbelief" (Matt. 13:58). The Nazarenes would not listen to His words or take Him seriously.

Faith comes by *hearing* the Word of God (Rom. 10:17). We don't have Jesus among us to teach and preach today, but He left us His living Word of Truth, which speaks directly to us. Whom do you hear teaching and preaching from the Word of Life? Are you connected to a church body and receiving a steady diet of the Word of Life? Do you really listen and soak it up, like water into a dry sponge, for applying to your life?

d. Being out of God's will. Wrong path. Wrong crowd. No righteous works. No abundant fruit, if any. No flow of the Spirit. Unresolved problems. Discouragement or other diabolical influences exerting themselves in your soul.

e. Sin, whether open or hidden, overt or subtle. Do you tithe, obey the Sabbath, give generously, honor your parents, maintain absolute loyalty to your spouse, produce righteous works by your faith, and love and pray for your enemies? Are you aware through your Bible study that the penalty for many types of these sins was physical death under the former Hebraic law of God?

God's character has not changed; the penalty for sin is still death. However, through the works of Jesus, we won't be dragged outside the city and stoned to death in this life! Spiritual death for sin will occur *after* our physical death.

f. Do you partake of communion periodically, symbolizing the drinking of Jesus' blood and eating of His flesh? There is spiritual power in this act of obedience, and you are doing this *in remembrance of Him* (and His great sacrifice on your behalf). How often do you remember Jesus and His sacrifice for you?

The first Church Body certainly understood the value of taking communion together. There is power in His name, power in His blood, and power available to us through His flesh having taken on all sin and disease for mankind. We have authority over demon spirits because of Jesus' victory over death, hell, and the grave. He triumphed that we may triumph in our mortal bodies.

g. Not recognizing Him when He speaks, by not being sensitive to Him, not making time to wait upon Him, or not hearing because of the background noise in your life. Regular Bible study and prayer give you ears to hear His voice. Waiting upon the Lord afterward allows Him to speak to you in a quiet environment. If you seek Him, you shall surely find Him!

h. Not being filled with His Spirit, an act which infuses power and which greatly ramps up the volume of His still small voice in your spirit, like an amplifier in a sound system.

It is within the believer's re-created, born-again human spirit that God's Spirit dwells. That is the pure and righteous part of a believer. From your spirit, the Holy Spirit guides, inspires, reveals, operates gifts of the Spirit, speaks with other tongues, gives spiritual dreams and visions, and brings forth all the other manifestations of God. It is out of your spirit that the Life of God, His truth, and His light go forth into the entire world. You are the vessel of His Spirit, His dwelling place on Earth, the modern-day holy temple of God. You are His priest, you have direct access to His presence at all times in prayer, and He no longer requires a tabernacle in the wilderness or a temple in Jerusalem with an ark and veil.

The works of Jesus removed those physical barriers to our relationship and communication with God. We are sons and daughters, engrafted into the true vine, and partakers of His righteousness through our new birth. Especially for us Gentiles, there is now light and life where only darkness and death existed before.

I state these wondrous things because they are not to be overlooked or undervalued by believers. If you *really* believe these statements, then you have the privilege of walking and talking with your Father on a daily basis, as did Adam, Enoch, Jesus, and many others before us. The key to hearing His voice is found in your spirit. Here are some helpful truths that will increase your ability to hear His voice and improve the clarity of His message.

- Build up your spirit by fasting and prayer. Have you ever seen a little plastic water aspirator that connects to the discharge end of a faucet? When the water is turned on and flows through the faucet, a negative pressure (vacuum) is created by the water flowing past an aspirator tube fitted onto the side of the plastic at ninety degrees. This aspirator is analogous to prayer and fasting for the believer; when the Spirit of God is flowing, prayer and fasting pulls you into the center of that flow!

- Strengthen your spirit and renew your mind (soul) by feeding on His Word. Plenty has already been said on this subject.

- Get your renewed soul in agreement with your spirit, and deny the carnal desires of the flesh. Your new spirit solely is the righteousness of God within you. Let it filter, guard, and govern your thoughts and imaginations, your carnal desires, and your motives. Bring these inherent areas of human weakness under the rulership of your spirit. You will find that you can control the desire to smoke, partake of food-lust, gaze at pornography, steal, lie, take drugs, and indulge in other harmful or illegal actions by doing as your spirit and soul agree, not as your flesh (body) desires to do.

   Your spirit will seek to obey God's Word, and it has the Holy Spirit within to guide it. The flesh is focused on self-gratification; the spirit is focused on doing what pleases the Father of Lights. God's Spirit works in tandem with your human spirit to make you a conqueror!

- Allow your spirit to outwardly produce fruit in your life: love, joy, peace, patience, kindness, goodness, faithfulness, gentleness, and self-control (Gal. 5:22). Many people mistakenly think that these are the fruits of God's Spirit within us. No, He already manifests these qualities! His Spirit works within our spirits to develop these *in us*. It is the human spirit that must develop fruit.

As we grow and mature in spiritual matters, we will begin to outwardly show *the fruit that develops within our spirits*. Why do you think Jesus spent so much time teaching in parables to His followers (not to unbelievers) that *they* must bear fruit in season, that others will judge *us* by our fruit, that by *our* fruit (especially love) men will know that we are followers of His?

Do you manifest these fruits consistently before your family, co-workers on the job, neighbors, and sports buddies? If not, you may be wondering why you don't hear God's voice or know what His will is for your life. How will you differentiate between an opportunity presented versus a trap laid by the enemy of your soul? How will you know if this strong feeling you are experiencing is a leading by God or a compulsion driven by a familiar spirit?

The exciting part for me is getting direction from God's Spirit in everyday life decision-making. However, I don't always stop and pray about each decision. I sometimes allow noise to drown out His voice, and I sometimes hear incompletely; so my spiritual antennae are not always at their optimum for knowing what God would have me do. However, I'm making steady progress in this vital area and hearing Him more frequently and more clearly.

Here's how God leads me (independent of other manifestations such as dreams, visions, prophecies) on a day-to-day basis. There is a close parallel to the Urim and Thummim's leading of the first orders of high priests, a description of which was covered in detail earlier. I pray about an issue, see what His Word says about it (if it is covered), and seek God's direction for a decision. As I pray and meditate (and fast at times, depending on the relative importance), I look to my spirit (which is where God's Spirit dwells) for direction, for either a "warm and fuzzy" feeling or for a check, or "stop," feeling.

The warm and fuzzy, velvety feeling in my spirit is like a green light indicating go. It feels like a release, with no resistance to going forward. A distinct feeling of void or absence of direction, or a check with a feeling of resistance that indicates restraint leads me to a no. As I look to my spirit for God's Spirit to direct me from there, I find that He is faithful to lead me in this manner. I still have to walk by faith and trust His leading. Like with all spiritual things, I have to *act* on my faith for results to materialize in the natural realm. The more I look to God's Spirit for direction, the easier it gets to recognize His form of yes or no. He may still show me things in dreams and visions, and He may choose to speak to me out of my spirit, but the typical day-to-day need for direction does not come in those forms.

The direction and consequences of this Spirit-leading should always be in agreement with God's Word, and when combined with effectual prayer, it will produce a greater walk of faith for the believer. The more you trust God and rely upon His leading, the more you will exercise faith in other areas of your life and in subsequent situations of needing direction. Remember, though, to consistently and sincerely adhere to the principles bulleted above when seeking direction from God's Spirit.

My first experience with hearing God's voice speaking to me live out of my spirit came in the early spring of 1976. My wife was in the third trimester of pregnancy with our second child. I had been working in a suit and tie all day in a hospital on a very hot day. When I was leaving to go home, both my car and I were hot as ovens. I got in the car, opened all the windows, turned the air conditioner on high, loosened my tie, turned on the radio, and headed home.

As I was listening to the music, singing along and cooling down fast in heavy traffic, suddenly a strong, clear voice spoke to me and broke through the atmosphere in the car. The voice said, "I am giving you a son." It shocked me at first, since I looked around and there was no one in the backseat. Then I realized that the voice was not audible; my ears had not heard a thing. The voice was coming from within my spirit! It was finished as quickly as the words had been spoken, and only those few words were said. The voice and the message certainly got my attention. I quickly turned off the radio and drove the rest of the way home almost in a daze, thinking about what happened and what was stated to me as fact.

At that time, it was not common for the expectant mother to get the sonograms during pregnancy that they now do, so we did not know the gender of the child as we drove to the hospital later for the delivery. When the nurses hooked up the fetal monitors and the doctor performed the continuous epidural anesthesia, all of them assured us that the baby was a healthy girl. I told them that I *knew* it would be a son, which got some chuckles in reply. They said they were the experienced ones, and the baby's signs showed a typical girl's pattern.

Until the delivery was completed, even during the remainder of labor and the majority of delivery, they teased me about my insistence that it would be a son. I took the ribbing good-naturedly because I *knew* that it was a boy. For the first time in my life, I was standing on the solid Rock, the sure foundation. God had spoken that word of wisdom to me several months earlier, and the reality of it still rang in my ears!

Then the baby popped the rest of the way out of the birth canal, and there was silence for a few moments as the medical staff saw a little baby boy. They looked at me, and no one knew what to say. I had been so firm in my conviction that it would be a boy, and they had been so mocking and teasing with me that the subject was now too awkward and was thus not mentioned again. If it had been, I was prepared to explain the source of my faith and how I *knew*. No one did ask or comment, but I left with a convincing lesson that God's Word is true and it stands on the Rock of my salvation, Jesus Christ.

It was a while longer before I experienced God's Spirit speaking to me like that again; but, He taught me a tremendous faith lesson from that experience and I began to learn what standing on His Word was all about, whether it was written in Scripture or spoken in the spirit realm. I learned that God's Word accepted by faith transcends human circumstances and even facts presented in the physical realm. The experience allowed me to also begin to look for and *expect* God to speak to me. That experience was a landmark in my spiritual growth. Now I always try to make time after prayer to wait upon the Lord, in case He has something to say. I encourage you to do the same.

Fruits of the Spirit

What joy there is in the realization that we can bear visible fruit for the Kingdom of God while on Earth, through both our maturation in spiritual growth and development and through our acting on our faith in good works! We are to be filled with the fruits of righteousness, which come out of our relationship with Jesus and are for the glory and praise of God (see Phil. 1:11).

There is a chapter following this one devoted to the subject of works, so I want to focus here on the various fruits of our spirits evident when yielding our lives to the transforming power of Jesus, His written Word, and His Holy Spirit. If He is not allowed to be Master and Lord of your life, these fruits will not be produced because the kernel will not have died in the soil so that the seed may germinate and bring forth abundant fruit in its season.

As a background to this subject, let's look at some Scriptures that illuminate our understanding of basic concepts of spiritual fruit.

- Matthew 7:15–20 NLT: Here Jesus was teaching the people extensively about spiritual principles and focused on fruit in people's lives.

  Beware of false prophets who come disguised as harmless sheep but are really vicious wolves. You can identify them by their fruit, that is, by the way they act. Can you pick grapes from thornbushes, or figs from thistles? A good tree produces good fruit, and a bad tree produces bad fruit. A good tree can't produce bad fruit, and a bad tree can't produce good fruit. So every tree that does not produce good fruit is chopped down and thrown into the fire. Yes, just as you can identify a tree by its fruit, so you can identify people by their actions.

- Luke 13:6–7 NLT: "Then Jesus told this story: 'A man planted a fig tree in his garden and came again and again to see if there was any fruit on it, but he was always disappointed. Finally, he said to his gardener, "I've waited three years, and there hasn't been a single fig! Cut it down. It's just taking up space in the garden." ' "

- John 15:5, 8, 16 NLT: "Yes, I am the vine; you are the branches. Those who remain in me, and I in them, will produce much fruit. For apart from me you can do nothing.... When you produce much fruit, you are my true disciples. This brings great glory to my Father.... You didn't choose me. I chose you. I appointed you to go and produce lasting fruit, so that the Father will give you whatever you ask for, using my name."

- John 12:24 NLT: Jesus here was explaining to His followers why He must die. We, too, must die—to self, to our carnal desires, to impure motives, and to pride—for new life in Christ to emerge from us and to bear fruit for His Kingdom. "I tell you the truth, unless a kernel of wheat is planted in the soil and dies, it remains alone. But its death will produce many new kernels—a plenteous harvest of new lives."

- Philippians 1:10–11 NLT: Paul doesn't have long to live (in prison in Rome) and writes these words to the church in Philippi: "For I want you to understand what really matters, so that you may live pure and blameless lives until the day of Christ's return. May you always be filled with the fruit of your salvation—the righteous character produced in your life by Jesus Christ—for this will bring much glory and praise to God."

• Galatians 5:22–23 NLT: Paul wrote to the churches in Galatia because of the controversies surrounding the relationship of new believers (including Gentiles) to the Jewish religious laws. Young converts needed to understand their freedom from the bondage to the Mosaic Law.

  This Scripture reads, "But the Holy Spirit produces this kind of fruit in our lives: love, joy, peace, patience, kindness, goodness, faithfulness, gentleness, and self-control. There is no law against these things!" The Holy Spirit works these qualities through our spirits, just as He speaks to us and operates gifts of the Spirit. These are a few of the fruits of our spirits, when we have yielded our souls and gotten them in line with our spirits.

  Many hear these familiar fruits read from Scripture and limit their understanding of spiritual fruit to just those in this passage. That is a big mistake! These are important, and they do reflect a point of maturity in our spiritual development when the Holy Spirit's nature has been acquired by our human spirits and those qualities then permeate our renewed minds (souls). However, reading through the rest of the New Testament reveals other basic expressions (fruits) of God in our daily lives that reflect the work accomplished by His Spirit in us: humility, meekness, service, stewardship, mercy, forgiveness, compassion, peacemaking, and others. These qualities do not come naturally to the base nature of unregenerate man. For them to be developed and expressed outwardly in believers requires the new birth, followed by death to self and ultimately by a progressive submission to the Holy Spirit and renewal of the soul (intellect, will, and emotions) by the Word of God.

This subject of fruit borne of a believer's ongoing transformation or maturation is a cornerstone of Jesus' teaching in the Gospels.

He stressed that there would be outward manifestations of the change that occurs when a believer becomes born again—all things become new (2 Cor. 5:17), the chains that had us bound in darkness are broken, we are brought into the light, we are forgiven of all sins, and our human spirits are re-created in purity and righteousness with no trace of the original Adamic sin.

Jesus also emphasized the true character traits that *emerge and impact others* when believers have died to self, made Him Lord of their lives, and have "put under" their bodies and souls. God purifies our spirits, but He does not purify our bodies and souls at the new birth. We must actively work to purify and to perfect both soul and body. Some believers don't ever start down that path of sanctification, and they remain carnal Christians, consumers of body resources, obstacles or hindrances to others, or ones who bring scorn and derision on the Christian walk from the ungodly.

When we subordinate the body and soul to the new regenerated spirit, God's Spirit can then manifest His nature through the human spirit for the world to see (and for the praise of the Father in Heaven). The Holy Spirit does not need to change; He already has the nature of God, and He bears all the fruit/nature/character of God. It is *we* who have to change in order to become of value (pure and fruitful) in His Army, His Body, and His Bride. By His grace, our spirit begins to mature and display the nature of God's Spirit as we commit to change our old ways and show the world His joy, meekness, gentleness, faithfulness, etc.

Our spirits must have the rule over our bodies and souls for God's nature to be expressed in us consistently and fully to the world. The more transformed the mind and the more submitted the body, the more God's character replaces the human instincts and base desires of our humanity—we are indeed changed creatures!

These outward godly traits flowing out of our individual human spirits to the world are the heart of this chapter on fruit. My prayer is that you are already bearing this fruit for the Kingdom of God on Earth as you have moved from being a new Christian to some advanced stage of spiritual development, purging your soul and body of unrighteousness and bringing forth new attitudes, character traits, and personality that reflect the perfecting process.

You cannot acquire these traits by sitting in a pew and getting them from the pulpit. They don't come to you by dropping down from Heaven, like a gift. You cannot acquire them by being passive toward Bible study and prayer. You must realize your need to grow and mature in spiritual things to be of value (works and fruit) in His Kingdom. "For the fruit of the Spirit is in all goodness and righteousness and truth" (Eph. 5:9).

A flower will never bloom if it does not get properly rooted, receive adequate moisture, obtain beneficial nutrients, and receive sunlight for its energy. Similarly, we have to root ourselves in the Word, be filled with His Spirit, be discipled and planted in His Church, and face the Son for our light and life.

Keep in mind how the Holy Spirit is always present to *help* us change from who we were to whom God desires us to be. It is by the choice and force of *our will* that change occurs. God does not coerce us to change anything. He is an absolute gentleman and is patient during our maturation process. But He expects change to occur. He draws and leads by His Spirit within us, His Word explains and encourages progressive change, and His character revealed to the world through our spirits validates us as His disciples.

Let's look at some other outward signs (fruits) that clearly show we have decided to change our base nature (soul and body) and acquire the nature of God. These Scriptures should speak loudly to each of us and act as mirrors for a close examination of ourselves.

- Matthew 5:41–45: "And whosoever shall compel thee to go a mile, go with him twain. Give to him that asketh thee, and from him that would borrow of thee turn not thou away. Ye have heard that it hath been said, Thou shalt love thy neighbor, and hate thine enemy. But I say unto you, Love your enemies, bless them that curse you, do good to them that hate you, and pray for them which despitefully use you, and persecute you; that ye may be the children of your Father which is in Heaven."

  These guidelines and commandments give you a basis for deciding how to respond to those who might ask something of you: the needy, panhandlers, beggars, neighbors, those having a hard time, those at risk, and people you might naturally despise or hate in the unregenerate state. But you are no longer in an unregenerate state and have no excuse for unrighteous behavior toward others! You are an ambassador for Christ; look like it, sound like it, and act like it wherever you are. Otherwise, your works are unfruitful and will be judged accordingly at the Judgment Seat of Christ.

- Matthew 6:1–18: These Scriptures cover our righteous approach and actions involved with tithing and giving, praying, forgiving others, and fasting. We are told the righteous way and the unrighteous way to act before people in these key areas of our daily walk as believers. How do you measure up? Are you truly forgiving toward all others at all times or just *selectively* forgiving, depending on what the transgression against you has been?

- John 13:34–35: "A new commandment I give unto you, That ye love one another; as I have loved you, that ye also love one another. By this shall all men know that ye are my disciples, if ye have love one to another."

  Do you allow God's unqualified and undeserved love for you to flow out from your spirit through a renewed, transformed soul and body to those around you in order to affect them for the Kingdom? If not, you are not yet His disciple.

  I think this is the hardest challenge we face as believers: giving unconditional love to others at work, in the neighborhood, among our relatives, at church, and in the sports/recreation arenas. This type of outward love is not our original base nature. We do not want to show love, especially to strangers or those we don't like or get along with easily. We tend to avoid people who aren't pleasant to us or who hate us, talk behind our backs, and embarrass us. Our churches need to spend time on this subject in practical discipleship classes. If we don't pass this litmus test of love, we don't qualify to be Jesus' disciples!

- Luke 8:14–15: Here Jesus is teaching on the parable of the seed, the Word of Truth, Himself: "And that which fell among thorns are they, which, when they have heard, go forth, and are choked with cares and riches and pleasures of this life, and *bring no fruit to perfection*. But that on the good ground are they, which in an honest and good heart, having heard the word, keep it, and *bring forth fruit with patience*" (emphasis added).

  If you are feeding on His Word and letting it transform your soul while actively choosing to turn away from carnal desires and ignore worldly distractions, you will be changed into His likeness; and this progression toward perfection of body and soul will result in your acquiring the mind of Christ and taking on His nature! You will be like a fig tree bearing its fruit in season, of much value to the Kingdom because you are successfully (and obediently) doing what you were called to do.

- John 15:1–2: A key Scripture for all believers to understand, it describes the Father's attitude toward those *believers* who are engrafted into Jesus, the true vine, at the new birth. However, it is not enough that we become part of the vine—we must then bear fruit, or the Father will cut us off altogether. Those who do bear fruit are contributing to the vine and will be pruned (instructed, chastised, and purified further) in order to bring forth maximum fruit.

  This is a sobering message to many believers, and I trust that the Holy Spirit will be able to deposit it into those who are not bearing fruit on the vine. Jesus said: "I am the true vine, and my Father is the husbandman. Every branch in me that beareth not fruit he taketh away: and every branch that beareth fruit, he purgeth it, that it may bring forth more fruit."

A study of spiritual fruit borne of good works and righteous stewardship would not be credible without looking into the life of Joseph, the great-grandson of Abraham. He was sensitive to God because his father, Jacob, and grandfather, Isaac, had discipled him from birth in the fear and love of El Shaddai (God had not revealed Himself yet to the Hebrews as Jehovah), telling him of the wondrous things God had done through and to their families.

Joseph trusted God as a very young man, as evidenced by the spiritual dreams he had faith in (for fulfillment in time). He endured the ridicule and jealousy of his ten older brothers because of his devotion to spiritual matters and his father Jacob's favor. However, these things were good, but not sufficient, to accomplish God's purposes in Joseph's life. Joseph had to be tested and proven faithful in the small things of his father Jacob's possessions before God could entrust him to produce fruit-bearing, righteous works in *great* things for the Kingdom.

God does the same with us today, waiting for us to prove faithful, sincere, obedient, and eager to please Him in utilizing what He puts into our hands to build His Kingdom. As we do serve Him in the least, He can then begin to entrust us with the *true riches*—spiritual gifts, anointings, spiritual blessings, supernatural visitations, and other deep things of His Spirit. He does not place these in the hands of those who would sit on them and not bear fruit for His Kingdom!

Turn to Genesis, chapters 39–50, and read how Joseph submitted himself and every Earthly possession and title given into his hands to the God of his fathers for the protection and growth of the Kingdom of God. (God's Kingdom on Earth was extremely small at this time; it consisted solely of the Hebrew families of Jacob, seventy members. The rest of the known world was in spiritual darkness, including Joseph's uncle Esau and all of that extended family.) Joseph never coveted others' property, he never took bribes or gifts in his positions of authority, and his response to questions about his growing stature always was to glorify God as his source. We are not told in Scripture that he accumulated wealth for himself; we are shown how he *used* his authority and *managed* possessions to accomplish God's revealed purposes.

These qualities had been developed over time through godly training by Isaac and Jacob until Joseph was ready to be the instrument of deliverance for the chosen Hebrew people of God, similar to the great deliverance by Moses several hundred years (430) later. Had it not been for Joseph's faith in God, his willingness to serve in his calling, his obedience to God's directions, and his abundant fruit produced from good works of faith, the few Hebrew people at that time would have died, and there would have been no Hebrew nation to conquer the land of Canaan and live under the covenant of God, no lineage to the Messiah, no ultimate sacrifice on Calvary, and certainly no hope for any of us Gentiles. Joseph was the only man standing between mankind's hope of salvation and the abyss. This is yet another foreshadowing in Scripture of the Messiah, the chosen one, who hung on a cross at Golgotha between Heaven and Earth for the salvation of mankind.

I am so thankful that Joseph was obedient and faithful in his lifetime of good stewardship, good works, and abundant fruit. In the next chapter on works, we will examine in more detail how Joseph is a paramount example of acting in faith by doing righteous works that bear good fruit for the glory of God. Are there people in darkness with no hope who are dependent on you to fulfill your calling in God and to bear abundant fruit in order for them to see the light of the gospel?

Importance of Works

As believers we must be people of faith in order for God to work His purposes through us. We receive a measure of faith at birth, and we build up that faith by *feeding on* the Word of Life, King Jesus Himself, and praying in the Spirit. We also get our faith built up *by hearing* the Word taught and preached (Rom. 10:17).

Picture in your mind a long-time Christian who studies the Word daily, is planted in the local church body of believers, who sits under the spiritual oversight and preaching of his pastor and ministry staff, and who prays diligently every day. Is that person actually maturing in the things of God and effecting change within his sphere of influence? He may be like so many others in today's typical church — sitting in the pew and getting fat on faith but never putting his faith into works for the Kingdom.

That kind of person is certainly a part of the Kingdom of God, at least for a while, but he is not laboring *to build* the Kingdom and *to produce good fruits* of righteousness that glorify God. In the previous chapter, we saw what Jesus said in John 15 about that type of person: he will be held accountable for his slothfulness, exhibited by his lack of good fruit! We are to be zealous of good works, showing in all things a pattern of good works, which will yield good fruit (Titus 2:7, 14).

In the previous chapter, I discussed the *fruit,* or results, of works, which can be either good or bad. The works themselves can be good or bad, determined by whether they are God-led or flesh-driven. In some cases, works may be demon-driven.

Paul warned Titus about men coming into the Church whose souls were defiled and who lacked faith to act: "They profess that they know God; but in works they deny him, being abominable and disobedient, and unto every good work reprobate" (Titus 1:16). Paul further stated in chapter 2 of Titus that we are to show a *pattern* of good works in all things and to be *zealous* of good works.

Jesus said that believers can look at the fruit of others and judge it, whether good (godly) or not. We can see their fruit and know how to pray for them. We are not to judge the heart or motives of another person. That responsibility is for Jesus alone.

Let's look at some Scriptures that allow us to view works from God's perspective, not from ours.

- James 2:14–26 NLT (emphasis added):

> What good is it, dear brothers and sisters, if you say you have faith but don't show it by your actions? Can that kind of faith save anyone? Suppose you see a brother or sister who has no food or clothing, and you say, "Good-bye and have a good day; stay warm and eat well"—but then you don't give that person any food or clothing. What good does that do? So you see, *faith by itself isn't enough.* Unless it produces good deeds, it is dead and useless. Now someone may argue, "Some people have faith; others have good deeds." But I say, "How can you show me your faith if you don't have good deeds? *I will show you my faith by my good deeds.*" You say you have faith, for you believe that there is one God. Good for you! Even the demons believe this, and they tremble in terror. How foolish! Can't you see that *faith without good deeds is useless?* Don't you remember that our ancestor Abraham was shown to be *right with God by his actions* when he offered his son Isaac on the altar? You see, his faith and his actions worked

together. *His actions made his faith complete.* And so it happened just as the Scriptures say: "Abraham believed God, and God counted him as righteous because of his faith." He was even called the friend of God. So you see, we are shown to be right with God *by what we do, not by faith alone.* Rahab the prostitute is another example. She was shown to be right with God by her actions when she hid those messengers and sent them safely away by a different road. Just as the body is dead without breath, so also *faith is dead without good works.*

These verses make understanding the importance of works as God's method of achieving change on Earth so easy, yet the enemy of our souls wants to keep mankind ignorant and lazy about this subject.

- Galatians 6:9: "And let us not be weary *in well doing:* for in due season we shall reap, if we faint not" (emphasis added). Do not get tired of doing good works; they are for a short season. and the rewards for good fruit are vast and eternal.

- Titus 3: 5, 8: "Not by works of righteousness which we have done, but according to his mercy he saved us.... that they which have believed in God might *be careful to maintain good works.* These things are *good and profitable* unto men" (emphasis added). You and I did not obtain salvation by anything good that we did. However, once saved we are expected to produce good works by acting on our faith.

- 2 Corinthians 5:7–10: "For we walk by faith, not by sight: We are confident, I say, and willing rather to be absent from the body, and to be present with the Lord. Wherefore *we labour,* that, whether present or absent, we may be accepted of him. For we must all appear before the Judgment Seat of Christ; that every one may receive the *things done in his body,* according to *that he hath done,* whether it be *good or bad"* (emphasis added).

- Ephesians 2:8–10: "For by grace are ye saved through faith; and that not of yourselves: it is the gift of God: Not of works, lest any man should boast. For we are his workmanship, *created in Christ Jesus unto good works,* which God hath before *ordained that we should walk in them"* (emphasis added).

- Romans 2:31–33: Paul is speaking in this letter and these verses to the church at Rome, teaching them about the issues and controversy surrounding new gentile converts. I like to link these verses with the one in Ephesians above for clarity on the issue of faith versus works. We will discuss the two different types of works in these similar verses to avoid any misunderstanding.
  "But Israel, which followed after the law of righteousness, hath not attained to the law of righteousness. Wherefore? Because they sought it not by faith, but as it were by the works of the law. For they stumbled at that stumblingstone; As it is written, Behold, I lay in Sion a stumblingstone and rock of offence: and whosoever believeth on him shall not be ashamed."

- 1 Corinthians 3:13–15: "Every man's work shall be made manifest: for the day shall declare it, because it shall be revealed by fire: and the fire shall try every man's work of what sort it is. If any man's work abide which he hath built thereupon, he shall receive a reward. If any man's work shall be burned, he shall suffer loss: but he himself shall be saved; yet so as by fire."

- Revelation 14:12–13: "Here is the patience of the saints: here are they that keep the commandments of God, and the faith of Jesus. And I heard a voice from Heaven saying unto me, Write, Blessed are the dead which die in the Lord from henceforth: Yea, saith the Spirit, that they may rest from their labours; and *their works do follow them"* (emphasis added).

A review of what these few verses tell us may make a huge difference in our lives and that of other Christians we know.

1. *We must accept Christ by faith.* The Jews in the new Church after the resurrection of Jesus were still struggling with obedience to the law given to Moses. Their works of the law were merely obedience to the law (animal blood sacrifices, special observances of feasts, rigid adherence to rites and ordinances and covenant requirements, enforcement of harsh penalties for violations) and would not get them to Jesus. They only pointed Israel to the coming Messiah. The Gentiles were accepting Jesus by faith, and Paul wanted all Jews to know that good news, that Jesus had fulfilled the requirements of the law and had made salvation, redemption, and atonement available through His own blood at Calvary.

2. *Once saved by the grace of God through Jesus, we must act on our faith, or else it is worthless going forward.* Faith without works is dead! These are not the works of the law; these are works of faith in Jesus.

3. *There are good works of faith, and there are bad works.* Only good works will bear fruit for the Kingdom of God.

4. *All Christians will be judged by their works (and the fruit they bear) at the Judgment Seat of Christ.* You will be rewarded or penalized eternally according to your works while in this brief life.

5. The good works that are done by Christian believers *continue* to follow them *after their death!* There are many examples of this reality throughout Scripture. One good work that follows generation after generation and keeps bearing good fruit is *disciple-*

ship. We will see this one and many other examples as we look closely at the works produced in Joseph's life.

Go in your Bible to Matthew 5:13–16 and see some examples of good works for the Kingdom that we all can easily do. These are described to the multitudes of new Christians by Jesus during the Sermon on the Mount, immediately following His description of godly characteristics that we call the Beatitudes. The illustrations that Jesus gives us here are the foundational works that we as Christians are expected to be achieving as believers in Christ in a world of spiritual darkness—we are salt and light within the world.

The passage reads: "Ye are the salt of the earth: but if the salt have lost his savour, wherewith shall it be salted? It is thenceforth good for nothing, but to be cast out, and to be trodden under foot of men. Ye are the light of the world. A city that is set on an hill cannot be hid. Neither do men light a candle, and put it under a bushel, but on a candlestick; and it giveth light unto all that are in the house. Let your light so shine before men, that they may see your good works, and glorify your Father which is in Heaven."

We are as *salt* among the mix of humanity, endued with special power from our Lord for affecting the ones in chains of spiritual darkness and for strengthening the Body of Christ. Think of our obligation to produce good works and bear fruit in this way as a commandment to be displaying the properties of salt: it preserves, it heals, it purifies, it adds flavor, and it certainly creates thirst.

Just as a small bit of yeast in dough can result in a huge quantity of bread, so can a little application of salt stop the process of progressive infection, promote healing, create excitement (enhance flavor), prevent decay, or produce a craving for water. This analogy is very clear in its benefits to building the Body of Christ on Earth: we want to bring the Bread of Life to fallen humanity so that He can restore mankind to God through His blood, heal bodies, deliver the oppressed, fill with His Spirit, and create a hunger/thirst for His living Word.

These qualities of salt, when applied to our daily walk, provide us with a natural progression of greater and greater influence on our families, our colleagues at work, our neighbors, and our various friends and acquaintances. This developing influence requires only baby steps for young converts to take, since the source of effect on others is the Holy Spirit within! Our efforts to achieve godly influence over others are good works that can bear great fruit.

I love Jesus' analogy of Christians as points of *light*. There are many Scriptures that tell us that God is the Father of Lights, that describe His brilliance in Heaven (making it the city of lights), that tell us Jesus is the Light of the World, and other references to divine light.

Our role is to be the light of the world in Jesus' absence. He now sits at the right hand of the Father, as our High Priest and Advocate. We are his ambassadors, full of His Spirit of light, and the source of light to the dying world in darkness. We are commissioned as soldiers to go forth and take the light of the gospel into darkness.

Keep in mind, however, that we are not judged purely by the results (numbers) of people accepting Jesus. We are to shine our light to all men and not hide it. The Holy Spirit will draw them to our light; some will come to the light like moths to a lightbulb in summer, while some will scurry back into the darkness, not wanting the light to expose their evil deeds.

The good works will produce good fruit of many types. Our obligation is to follow the leading of the Holy Spirit and live our faith openly for the Kingdom. We are to be judged and rewarded on *what we did that He called us to do,* not merely on what we did, and on the purity of our motives and tactics. The ultimate end point of bearing good fruit for the Kingdom is that the Father receives glory and honor!

There is also a group of works that we typically limit our thinking of them solely to the ministry offices (pastor, evangelist, teacher, etc.) in the local church – laying on of hands in prayer for the sick, deliverance ministry, discipleship training, visiting the infirm, etc. Nevertheless, these works are the works of Jesus, and He has given to *all* His disciples the necessary provisions to do these good works. In addition to those works done at a higher level of ministry by those called of God, these works can be done on a regular basis at a lower level of responsibility to anyone we meet who is in need of the Master's touch.

We are equipped, but are we prepared *to act* on His Word in doing the works of Jesus? Unfortunately, in today's typical church, believers don't take these words to heart, and many churches wrongly teach that these works were *only* for the early Church and limited in application to the first apostles. Let's examine Matthew 10:1, 7–9, 10, 16, 19–20, 22, 27, 38–39.

> And when he had called unto him his twelve disciples, he gave them power against unclean spirits, to cast them out, and to heal all manner of sickness and all manner of disease.... And as ye go, preach, saying, The Kingdom of Heaven is at hand. Heal the sick, cleanse the lepers, raise the dead, cast out devils: freely ye have received, freely give. Provide neither gold, nor silver, nor brass in your purses.... for the workman is worthy of his meat.... Behold, I send you forth as sheep in the midst of wolves: be ye therefore wise as serpents, and harmless as doves.... But when they deliver you up, take no thought how or what ye shall speak: for it shall be given you in that same hour what ye shall speak. For it is not ye that speak, but the Spirit of your Father which speaketh in you.... And ye shall be hated of all men for my name's sake: but he that endureth to the end shall be saved.... What I tell you in darkness, that speak ye in light: and what ye hear in the ear, that preach ye upon the housetops.... And he that taketh not his cross, and followeth after me, is not worthy of me. He that findeth his life shall lose it: and he that loseth his life for my sake shall find it.

Have you been preparing yourself for doing these kinds of good works? Jesus has *provided all* the tools necessary for His Body to mobilize and take the world for His Kingdom. Unfortunately, this type of thinking is too radical for most churches and many believers prefer to sit in an air-conditioned church, wearing their Sunday best and hearing a nice, unchallenging, positive message before going to lunch on Sundays. They never seem to get motivated for doing the works of Christ that we are commissioned as disciples to do.

If this describes the level of teaching and preaching in your church, flee! Put yourself under the anointed ministry of a person who is not timid about declaring the full gospel of God and feeding the sheep a wholesome diet. If you don't sit under the right teaching or feed regularly on the Word of Truth *yourself,* you will feel inadequate for the job and resign yourself to just being a good Christian waiting for Jesus to return and take you to Heaven for eternity. That event will come, but we have a job, a direct commission of Jesus, to do His works while here on planet Earth.

Some people are called to do much more than others; for example, some believers are called to a ministry office and given special anointings, and all of us are each called to be an effective witness of Him. The provisions are there, regardless of the level or type of calling, and each believer is called for doing good works for the Kingdom.

Jesus did not give anything special to His contemporary disciples that He didn't also give to all disciples of His, for all eras and ages to come. He gave us His name and all the authority behind it; He gave us His Word of Life (our daily bread); He filled us with the Holy Spirit (who operates the gifts of the Spirit and other orchestrations on our behalves); and He gave all other necessary provision for any need that might arise when we represent Him before mankind.

Look at verses 9 and 10 of Matthew 10 as stated above: Jesus instructed His disciples to not even take money with them when they went out to do His works. Why? Look at verse 16: He told them to be wise, but harmless. How? Look at verses 19–20, 27: He said the disciples would be given direction, the Holy Spirit would provide the utterance for defense, and the disciples would be told what to say to the world. How?

These questions I've raised are answered mostly by verses 38 and 39: by His disciples following Jesus all the way to Calvary, losing their personal lives and individual identities *within Him,* spending time before the Father in prayer, resisting Satan, fasting, feeding on the Word of Truth, being filled with the Holy Spirit and walking in His power and gifts, seeking a deeper walk with Him than that of a young believer, and thirsting for outpourings and special anointings of the Spirit among people. You will have to be filled with His Spirit and spend time learning how to hear with hearing ears and yielding your body's vocal capabilities to the Holy Spirit for these things to occur in your life. Otherwise, you'll be in trouble (on your own) if you can't follow His leading or hear His voice or let Him speak through you in times of need.

Let's look at one fine example of a Bible believer who died to self in order to accomplish the good works that he was called to do for the glory of God. I briefly described the qualities of Joseph in the last chapter, but his good works were awesome in their long-lasting effects for God's Kingdom on Earth, which at the time was comprised of only seventy people. Joseph and his works provided a beautiful foreshadowing of Jesus and allowed the nation of Israel (Jacob, his father) to be nurtured, to multiply exceedingly in people and animals, and to become wealthier than probably any other group of people in history.

Turn to look at Genesis 39 through Exodus 1. God used Joseph to achieve many monumental tasks, all of which brought enormous glory to God, both then and for hundreds of years into the future. Some background and commentary on Egypt and God's people at this time period are discussed below.

1. Beginning with Abraham, the few Hebrews who existed had periodically needed to travel into Egypt for provisions, mainly because of drought or famine in Canaan. There were a number of back-and-forth visits. God enriched Abraham several times by these visits. However, for some reason it became an abomination for an Egyptian to eat with or to eat close to a Hebrew. We are not told what led to this separation. A guess on my part is that it had to do with the idolatrous Egyptians being offended by the Hebrews' blessing of the food prior to eating. I can also see it as a type of rejection by the world of the spiritual food (Bread of Life) eaten by believers.

2. In like manner, it had also become an abomination in Egypt for a man or family to shepherd flocks of sheep. Egypt was cattle country. Their basis for sustenance and their willing-

ness to spend time among the animals cared for were very, very different from that of the Hebrews. Cattle don't require much personal attention, but sheep do! Shepherding sheep was the primary occupation of the Hebrew families. This shepherding occupation is the analogy used most often by Jesus to describe His relationship (and that of His ministers) to His flock of sheep in His fold. He protects us, nurtures us, and guides us to greener pastures. Sheep will follow a good shepherd, but cattle have to be driven.

3. Pharaoh was not an absolute ruler and did not own or control the people, the cattle herds, or the lands of Egypt when Joseph arrived. He was not worshipped as a deity. The cult of royal deity had apparently not begun yet, although the seeds had been sown. He was allowed special places of honor, had a royal family burial area, and had cities and monuments named after him and his forefathers, as we still do with heads of state today. Similar to the kings and queens of England, Pharaoh was royalty and his family was a dynasty. However, he was the official head of state for Egyptian affairs whereas in England the queen or king is not the head of state in government.

4. Pharaoh, placed in power by God for His purposes, acknowl-edged the Hebrew God El Shaddai, recognized His power, and welcomed the Hebrews into Egypt, giving them the best of the Egyptian lands: the fertile Nile Delta known as the land of Goshen, which was under the control of the royal family and was also known as the land of Ramses. Pharaoh gave the Hebrews prime real estate (of his family), luxury accommodations, and the best supplies.

5. Pharaoh allowed Israel (Jacob) to bless him in the Hebrew manner ordained by God, which was up close and personal, according to the way God had taught Adam and all succeeding generations of godly men. This seems highly irregular and yet was an indication of how open this particular pharaoh

was to the ways of the Hebrew God and His people. This ruler was truly blessed of God and prospered under the good works of Joseph's hands.

6. The royal priesthood was established already in Egypt. It had been given a section of dedicated land for its exclusive use, and the priests' food and material needs were supplied by the pharaoh on the throne. In return, the priests were continuous servants to Pharaoh in the court, serving in a variety of functions: priestly duties between Pharaoh and their gods (including the chief sun god, Ra), observers and interpreters of the constellations in the sky, diviners, and spiritual counselors for guidance.

   It is quite obvious in Scripture that neither Joseph nor any of his family was ever accepted by or had a relationship with any of the priests of the land. I am sure that they saw his quickly rising status, fame, and wealth as a threat to their power, since Pharaoh began looking to Joseph for his personal counsel on matters of state and guidance as well as entrusting the protection of his nation into Joseph's hands. The natural enmity between the royal priests of Egypt and the Hebrews (and their God) was a reflection of the reality of good in the midst of evil and of light entering darkness.

   One thing to keep in mind was the growing spiritual power, although evil, of this royal priesthood. Satan himself must have positioned his Earth-based kingdom directly over Egypt during this time, being the prince of the air over this area of geography, to be adjacent to the promised land of Canaan and to work evil behind the scenes to prevent the lineage of Jacob from producing the future Lamb of God.

Joseph's works in obedience to God's direction were outstanding, and God used him not only to preserve the Hebrew people, but also to set up Egypt for the future deliverance of His people. Let's focus on some of Joseph's works and see how God's people benefited from his effective service to God and the resulting fruits. In a foreshadowing of things to come, the period of time that the Hebrews were in Egypt parallels the time period that Jesus was in the wilderness being tempted of Satan. It was a time of testing and calling upon God, praying and fasting for strength and direction. And in both situations, the future of God's people on Earth rested in the balance!

1. Genesis 39:2–6:

> And the Lord was with Joseph, and he was a prosperous man; and he was in the house of his master the Egyptian. And his master saw that the Lord was with him, and that the Lord made all that he did to prosper in his hand. And Joseph found grace in his sight, and he served him: and he made him overseer over his house, and all that he had he put into his hand. And it came to pass from the time that he had made him overseer in his house, and over all that he had, that the Lord blessed the Egyptian's house for Joseph's sake; and the blessing of the Lord was upon all that he had in the house, and in the field. And he left all that he had in Joseph's hand; and he knew not ought he had, save the bread which he did eat. And Joseph was a goodly person, and well favored.

The Lord was with Joseph because Joseph had been discipled by godly men, believed in El Shaddai as his personal and family's God, and was consistently obedient in doing good works that God showed or told him to do. He walked in righteousness, an upright young man, in spite of the character flaws exhibited by his ten older brothers. When trapped and sold by his brothers to alien traders, he didn't harbor hate and resentment, as many of today's Christians might be tempted to do.

How and why did Joseph prosper when sold into bondage in Egypt by the Ishmaelites? He prospered because he had the favor of God, and God gave Joseph favor with all men, regardless of the circumstances. God also was able to use

Joseph in things supernatural both in channel and result. How did this prosperity manifest itself? Joseph was given authority, privilege, and responsibilities among men that exceeded his situational position in life.

He had been bought by Potiphar as a young Hebrew slave, yet Potiphar recognized God's hand upon Joseph, saw that everything Joseph did prospered by the hand of God, and gave Joseph complete control of all his property and possessions, except for his wife. As God prospered Joseph's stewardship of Potiphar's property and it multiplied, Potiphar trusted Joseph so much that he let Joseph alone keep the books and didn't keep track any longer of his current assets. This incredible account shows how Joseph's obedience and good works began a lifetime of bringing glory to God.

2. Genesis 39:21–23:

> But the Lord was with Joseph, and shewed him mercy, and gave him favour in the sight of the keeper of the prison. And the keeper of the prison committed to Joseph's hand all the prisoners that were in the prison; and whatsoever they did there, he was the doer of it. The keeper of the prison looked not to any thing that was under his hand; because the Lord was with him, and that which he did, the Lord made it to prosper.

Next, Joseph found himself in a dire situation, thrown into prison under attempted rape charges, having lost his position over the property of the captain of Pharaoh's guard. This turned out to be a big promotion, since God used Joseph in the new environment to take charge over all the prisoners, again as a result of the prison keeper's recognition of God in Joseph's good works, prospering everything he did. Think of the risk to the prison keeper if his new prison trustee made a mistake or allowed a prisoner to break out: he would be put to death! God was working mightily in Joseph's life because

He had called him to do mighty works. God's direction of Joseph in prison (through prayer and his obedience in doing what God instructed and interpreted) would ultimately lead directly to Pharaoh's throne.

3. Genesis 41:37–41:

> And the thing was good in the eyes of Pharaoh, and in the eyes of all his servants. And Pharaoh said unto his servants, Can we find such a one as this is, a man in whom the Spirit of God is? And Pharaoh said unto Joseph, Forasmuch as God hath shewed thee all this, there is none so discreet and wise as thou art: Thou shalt be over my house, and according unto thy work shall all my people be ruled: only in the throne will I be greater than thou. And Pharaoh said unto Joseph, See, I have set thee over all the land of Egypt.

How brilliant of God to have set up this opportunity for Joseph to gain the highest favor of Pharaoh! God gave Joseph interpretations of dreams, and God provided Pharaoh with the dreams that would determine the destiny of both the Egyptian and Hebrew nations. Notice that Pharaoh recognized the hand of El Shaddai in Joseph's good works and wanted *that kind* of man to serve him and to rule over his people's land. Pharaoh then gave Joseph his signet ring to use, which meant that Joseph could act in place of Pharaoh in an official capacity to create laws, sign treaties, negotiate trade deals, and so forth.

Joseph was much more than an ambassador of the Egyptian government; as *governor* he *ruled over* everything in government in the land, directly under and accountable only to Pharaoh. This was divine intervention and favor by God for His ultimate purposes, as we will see later. It required, though, a vessel yielded and righteous for His use.

Joseph was consistently proving himself to be that doer of good works for the Father and bringing glory to God through

Pharaoh's own lips. Joseph's lack of need for Pharaoh's royal priests to provide the kinds of spiritual services and guidance to him as they provided for Pharaoh would build a wedge of bitterness between them and him, to be manifested later in open rebellion by the evil, demon-fraternizing, and self-serving priests against the Hebrews.

4. Genesis 45:16–20:

> And the fame thereof was heard in Pharaoh's house, saying, Joseph's brethren are come: and it pleased Pharaoh well, and his servants. And Pharaoh said unto Joseph, Say unto thy brethren, This do ye; lade your beasts, and go, get you unto the land of Canaan; And take your father and your households, and come unto me: and I will give you the good of the land of Egypt, and ye shall eat the fat of the land. Now thou art commanded, this do ye; take you wagons out of the land of Egypt for your little ones, and for your wives, and bring your father, and come. Also regard not your stuff; for the good of all the land of Egypt is yours.

Pharaoh and his administrative staff were excited to hear that Joseph's family was coming to Egypt. Not only that, but Pharaoh insisted that Joseph's brothers accept his luxury provisions to go after and bring back from Canaan all of their extended family of Hebrews who worshipped El Shaddai. Pharaoh told Joseph not to be concerned for his belongings, properties, and stuff; all the goods of the land of Egypt would be available to him and his family when the group returned. That was quite a dramatic life-change for a man who had arrived in Egypt as a penniless slave bought from traders who was now administrative governor of all the land.

5. Genesis 46:2–4:

> And God spake unto Israel in the visions of the night,
> and said, Jacob, Jacob. And he said, Here am I. And
> he said, I am God, the God of thy father: fear not to
> go down into Egypt; for I will there make of thee a
> great nation: I will go down with thee into Egypt;
> and I will also surely bring thee up again: and Joseph
> shall put his hand upon thine eyes.

God had to persuade Jacob (Israel) that He was behind
this Hebrew family move to Egypt. Israel knew well the
origins and direction by God of his grandfather, Abraham,
and the moves made by his father, Isaac. But Israel was old
and very settled in the land promised as an everlasting covenant with God, the land of Canaan.

God assured him that He was behind the move to Egypt,
that it would be for just a season, that He would accompany
him into Egypt, and that He would bring him (his seed) back
out again to Canaan. On top of those assurances, God made
Israel a prophetic promise that He would make a great nation
out of him while there in Egypt. We aren't told in Scripture
whether Israel asked for clarification about his return to
Canaan and the making of a great nation in Egypt, but we
know that God's plan was enormous in vision for Israel and
the Hebrews, all contingent on the continued obedience and
good works of one man, Joseph.

6. Genesis 47:5–7, 10–12:

> And Pharaoh spake unto Joseph, saying, Thy father
> and thy brethren are come unto thee: The land of
> Egypt is before thee; in the best of the land make thy
> father and brethren to dwell; in the land of Goshen let
> them dwell: and if thou knowest any men of activity
> among them, then make them rulers over my cattle.
> And Joseph brought in Jacob his father, and set him

before Pharaoh: and Jacob blessed Pharaoh.... And Jacob blessed Pharaoh, and went out from before Pharaoh. And Joseph placed his father and his brethren, and gave them a possession in the land of Egypt, in the best of the land, in the land of Rameses, as Pharaoh had commanded. And Joseph nourished his father, and his brethren, and all his father's household, with bread, according to their families.

Pharaoh decreed that Joseph and all of the Hebrew families, seventy in total number, should settle in *the best, most productive* part of Egypt: Goshen. That fertile delta land was prime land for animal grazing and farming because of the silt accumulations from the Nile River that emptied into the adjacent Mediterranean Sea. In Goshen, Pharaoh had his own cattle herds, and the royal dynasty had a sacred area where a previous pharaoh, Rameses, had come from and/or was buried.

This type of recognition of the Hebrew Joseph and his contribution in good works to the country was supernaturally inspired. Now here is a beautiful situation that was also divinely ordained: Pharaoh entertained Jacob (Israel) in his court as the older man was set before Pharaoh's throne. There Jacob prayed God's blessing upon this benevolent head of state for all to witness. Pharaoh received that blessing and prospered greatly, I'm sure, while placing the Hebrews in the best strategic position to prosper abundantly and multiply exceedingly.

We are not told so, but I am certain that the royal priests must have been silently shrieking in horror when watching Pharaoh receive the Hebrew blessing of El Shaddai. The prince of the air must have been quite upset too, although he could not have foreseen the great plan of God that was emerging through these extraordinary events. Only a loving God could arrange such a unique and ideal circumstance several thousand years ago for the benefit of all mankind today.

7. Genesis 47:14–17:

> And Joseph gathered up all the money that was found
> in the land of Egypt, and in the land of Canaan, for
> the corn which they bought: and Joseph brought
> the money into Pharaoh's house. And when money
> failed in the land of Egypt, and in the land of Canaan,
> all the Egyptians came unto Joseph, and said, Give
> us bread: for why should we die in thy presence?
> for the money faileth. And Joseph said, Give your
> cattle; and I will give you for your cattle, if money
> fail. And they brought their cattle unto Joseph: and
> Joseph gave them bread in exchange for horses, and
> for the flocks, and for the cattle of the herds, and for
> the asses: and he fed them with bread for all their
> cattle for that year.

When famine came to that part of the world, as God
had told Joseph earlier to place him in position, crops failed
and people from all around Egypt and from Canaan came
to Joseph to buy corn. By his obedience to God's direction,
Joseph had planted additional land in corn and had stored it
in city granaries during the previous seven years of plenty.
Joseph collected the huge quantities of currencies brought in
and gave the money to Pharaoh's accountants. As an upright
man, he kept none for himself and was transparent in all his
dealings for Pharaoh.

Then as the famine continued, people had no more
money to buy corn. All the money was now in Pharaoh's
treasury. God directed Joseph to begin accepting the people's
animal stock for the corn. For a year, Joseph collected all
the animals in the land and gave them to Pharaoh's staff for
handling. He had plenty of grain to feed all the animals now
in Pharaoh's enlarged stocks. So now Pharaoh owned all the
corn, all the money, and all the animal stock in Egypt! There
was a major transfer of power occurring in Egypt, from the

common people to the ruler, Pharaoh, as God worked His plan through His servant Joseph.

8. Genesis 47:19–20, 24–27:

> Wherefore shall we die before thine eyes, both we and our land? Buy us and our land for bread, and we and our land will be servants unto Pharaoh: and give us seed, that we may live, and not die, that the land be not desolate. And Joseph bought all the land of Egypt for Pharaoh; for the Egyptians sold every man his field, because the famine prevailed over them: so the land became Pharaoh's.... And it shall come to pass in the increase, that ye shall give the fifth part unto Pharaoh, and four parts shall be your own, for seed of the field, and for your food, and for them of your households, and for food for your little ones. And they said, Thou hast saved our lives: let us find grace in the sight of my lord, and we will be Pharaoh's servants. And Joseph made it a law over the land of Egypt unto this day, that Pharaoh should have the fifth part; except the land of the priests only, which became not Pharaoh's. And Israel dwelt in the land of Egypt, in the country of Goshen; and they had possessions therein, and grew, and multiplied exceedingly.

This story keeps getting more exciting as you read through it, for it was a well-orchestrated series of moves by God to simultaneously multiply and enrich the Hebrews while amassing total power in the hands of Egypt's ruler. Remember that this pharaoh was a wise, God-fearing, blessed, benevolent ruler who provided the best for God's people. He was delighted that the families of his beloved and highly respected governor, Joseph, were eating the fat of the land and abounding in all areas of life in the land of Goshen. God used this pharaoh to accomplish His purposes, just as

He used Joseph as the mover and shaker of His plans and the generator of all glory to El Shaddai across Egypt.

Now, money was gone, and the people had sold all their animals for corn. There was nothing left to barter for corn except their land and themselves. In desperation, all the people of Egypt sold their properties and became slaves to Pharaoh for more corn to stay alive. Joseph bought all the land of Egypt for Pharaoh!

However, Joseph had obediently stored such a huge inventory of grain during the plenteous years that he now could give the people grain to plant the land with seed for new crops. God was telling Joseph what to do and how to time each stage of the transfer of wealth and power into Pharaoh's hand. Joseph knew from the dreams of Pharaoh precisely when the famine would end. Therefore, he knew when to instruct the people to plant corn for new crops.

Joseph also established a new law for the ruler's slaves: they must give back to Pharaoh 20 percent of the crop harvest. (And some believers think it hard to pay God 10 percent of their harvest.) The royal priests were excluded from this law since they retained their ownership of the land given to them by Pharaoh; they didn't farm, they never had to buy corn or barter for it, and Pharaoh supplied all their Earthly needs from his own resources.

To recap, Pharaoh now owned everything and everybody in Egypt, except for the Hebrews and the royal priests, and got a continuous 20 percent revenue stream coming in from the crops planted by *his* people on *his* lands. The position and title of pharaoh had now become one of absolute ruler, dictator for life, holding total power over all Egypt.

Meanwhile, the Hebrews were rapidly populating the land of Goshen, accumulating wealth independently of the Egyptian people, living a life of plenty, enjoying the blessings of God, and being protected by both the benevolent pharaoh and his Hebrew governor. On the sidelines, the emasculated royal priests were sullenly watching the changes unfold without being directly involved in either

Pharaoh's administration of vast new power or the dramatic increase of the Hebrews and their strong spiritual influence for God over Pharaoh. As a result of the fruitful works of His servant Joseph, God had successfully set the stage for future confrontation.

Are you a righteous and obedient servant of God, doing the works of His calling in your life and bearing much fruit? God has only His people to use in accomplishing His plans on Earth.

9. Genesis 49:22–26:

> Joseph is a fruitful bough, even a fruitful bough by a well; whose branches run over the wall: The archers have sorely grieved him, and shot at him, and hated him: But his bow abode in strength, and the arms of his hands were made strong by the hands of the mighty God of Jacob; (from thence is the shepherd, the stone of Israel:) Even by the God of thy father, who shall help thee; and by the Almighty, who shall bless thee with blessings of Heaven above, blessings of the deep that lieth under, blessings of the breasts, and of the womb: The blessings of thy father have prevailed above the blessings of my progenitors unto the utmost bound of the everlasting hills: they shall be on the head of Joseph, and on the crown of the head of him that was separate from his brethren.

Joseph's father, Israel, was about to die in old age, and God instructed him to bring his twelve sons together and to prophesy over each one of them, telling them what would occur in their lives and for generations after them. In these verses, we read what was spoken through Israel over Joseph. It is a moving prophecy that acknowledges the obedient works of Joseph that brought much glory to God, and it foreshadows the future savior of mankind.

Joseph was described by God as not just a fruitful bough, but one growing by a well, continuously watered and sustained in strength through all seasons. He endured some hard times, but he was strong in God and able to accomplish God's purposes. Joseph was driven by God's calling on his life and did not allow circumstances, feelings, or evil schemes to sidetrack or limit him in doing the works of God. Untold varieties of blessing would be on Joseph and his heirs because of his faithfulness and fruitfulness.

10. Genesis 50:2–9:

> And Joseph commanded his servants the physicians to embalm his father: and the physicians embalmed Israel. And forty days were fulfilled the days of those which are embalmed: and the Egyptians mourned for him threescore and ten days. And when the days of his mourning were past, Joseph spake unto the house of Pharaoh, saying, If now I have found grace in your eyes, speak, I pray you, in the ears of Pharaoh, saying, My father made me swear, saying, Lo, I die: in my grave which I have digged for me in the land of Canaan, there shalt thou bury me. Now therefore let me go up, I pray thee, and bury my father, and I will come again. And Pharaoh said, Go up, and bury thy father, according as he made thee swear. And Joseph went up to bury his father: and with him went up all the servants of Pharaoh, the elders of his house, and all the elders of the land of Egypt, And all the house of Joseph, and his brethren, and his father's house: only their little ones, and their flocks, and their herds, they left in the land of Goshen. And there went up with him both chariots and horsemen: and it was a very great company.

The continued fruit borne of Joseph's obedient and consistent works is astounding. We see here that Israel died and was embalmed using the advanced technology of the Egyptians to preserve his body for the long trip back to Canaan for burial. This required forty days of work. All the land of Egypt mourned for Israel for seventy days, an official period of state mourning such as would honor a member of royalty.

When asked by Joseph for leave from his duties in Egypt to return to his homeland and bury his father, which would require some extended time, Pharaoh was not worried that Joseph would stay there and not return. Pharaoh was not concerned that Joseph's huge staff would prove incompetent in his absence and things begin to unravel with all the newly acquired animals, properties, and farming programs Pharaoh had acquired through Joseph during the famine. No, he knew from experience that Joseph had God's blessing upon him and that all his works would continue to bear fruit in his absence!

Pharaoh went even further; he insisted that there be a great procession of Egyptian nobles attending the burial to honor Israel. Pharaoh sent all his personal servants, all his house staff, and all the administrators from across Egypt to join with all the Hebrews. Furthermore, Pharaoh sent along a contingent of chariots and horsemen for protection and honor. The sight of this huge caravan of people and their supplies for the round trip must have put fear into the hearts of all the Canaanite tribes along the way! Several hundred years later (430, to be exact), they would confront true fear when God Himself led the Israelite nation out of Egypt.

11. Genesis 50:18–24:

> And his brethren also went and fell down before his face; and they said, Behold, we be thy servants. And Joseph said unto them, Fear not: for am I in the place of God? But as for you, ye thought evil against me; but God meant it unto good, to bring to pass, as it is this day, to save much people alive. Now there-

fore fear ye not: I will nourish you, and your little ones. And he comforted them, and spake kindly unto them. And Joseph dwelt in Egypt, he, and his father's house: and Joseph lived an hundred and ten years. And Joseph saw Ephraim's children of the third generation: the children also of Machir the son of Manasseh were brought up upon Joseph's knees. And Joseph said unto his brethren, I die: and God will surely visit you, and bring you out of this land unto the land which he sware to Abraham, to Isaac, and to Jacob.

Hebrews 11:22:

By faith Joseph, when he died, made mention of the departing of the children of Israel; and gave commandment concerning his bones.

Several noteworthy things are contained in these verses, all because Joseph always trusted God and followed His direction in blind faith, regardless of what his brothers, his Hebrew brethren, or his fame in Egypt brought about. He did not allow circumstances to dictate his works, and he did not proceed without seeking God's will.

Now, Israel was dead, buried in Canaan, and all the Hebrew nation was back in Egypt. Joseph's brothers started to worry because they had not risen above circumstances in life or learned that Joseph was a forgiving man of God. They were fearful that Joseph would imprison or kill them since Israel was gone. They fell down at his feet, professing their allegiance to him. This scene validated the spiritual dream given to the boy Joseph by God many years earlier in Canaan: the elder brothers would bow down before the younger and serve him. Of course, Joseph graciously accepted his brothers and confirmed to them his love and care for them and their families.

Joseph also had pondered in his heart, in faith, that which God had promised him—a return of His people and Joseph's bones to the promised land of Canaan—and he shared that covenantal promise with his family. Joseph didn't refer to carrying his *body* back to Canaan, only his *bones,* because God had already told him the things yet to transpire for His chosen people. When deliverance out of Egypt would commence exactly 430 years later, there would be no flesh remaining on Joseph's bones. Only his bones would be carried back for burial in the Promised Land.

Notice also the important scriptural reference to his progeny, all the way to his great-great-grandchildren; *Joseph discipled them* as children (on his knees) in the things of God, just as his father, Israel, and his grandfather, Isaac, had discipled him as a child. This process of discipleship and its continuity through generations of believers are critical factors in young people's bearing good fruit for the Kingdom of God.

12. Exodus 1:6–9, 11–12:

> And Joseph died, and all his brethren, and all that generation. And the children of Israel were fruitful, and increased abundantly, and multiplied, and waxed exceeding mighty; and the land was filled with them. Now there arose up a new king over Egypt, which knew not Joseph. And he said unto his people, Behold, the people of the children of Israel are more and mightier than we.... Therefore they did set over them taskmasters to afflict them with their burdens. And they built for Pharaoh treasure cities, Pithom and Raamses. But the more they afflicted them, the more they multiplied and grew. And they were grieved because of the children of Israel.

The original plan of God was now becoming obvious; the later-generation pharaohs were now supremely powerful (because of Joseph) and deluded by the prince of the air in a cult of deity. There were no God-pleasing Hebrews in government, so it seems. The Hebrews were so great in numbers, animals, and wealth in Goshen that there was both jealousy and paranoia toward them by the royal Egyptian family. The prosperity of the Hebrews was coveted by the wealthy royal family.

I am sure that the royal priests were plotting and agitating for dominance over the Hebrews, since their power had been ignored and unneeded during the administration of Joseph. They had kept their black arts under wraps while waiting for their return to power and great influence over the royal family. As happened, the Egyptian pharaohs changed the laws of Joseph, confiscated all the Hebrew properties and possessions, and placed the Hebrews under oppressive slavery. The pot of affliction was now boiling!

13. Romans 9:17: "For the scripture saith unto Pharaoh, Even for this same purpose have I raised thee up, that I might shew my power in thee, and that my name might be declared throughout all the earth."

Looking several thousand years ahead, we see that the Messiah came to Israel, died, and salvation (and spiritual freedom) was made available to all men upon the Earth. Paul writes under God's anointing that mighty Pharaoh, under whose hands the Hebrews toiled without mercy for many years, was merely a stooge, or puppet, in God's elaborate plan to demonstrate His power *to all nations* through miraculous deliverance of His people. These things were all possible because of the fruit borne of good works by one faithful man: Joseph, son of Israel.

In like manner, Jesus did the same much later; He brought glory to God throughout all the Earth by deliverance of all people in bondage to Satan and brought them into the promised land of Canaan (Heaven). This parallel is so beautiful because God set up the circumstances for both men to come on the scene and achieve great things for His glory in such a short time period for all people and at the expense of the dominant powers on Earth at the time.

What is God preparing today? Who is listening to His calling and being obedient and righteous for His use? Let us all learn much from the history of Joseph as a yielded vessel through whom God achieved much glory through fruitful works.

Walking in the Spirit

This final chapter looks at the typical Christian who seeks to please God by acting on faith, by doing good works, and bearing good fruit in season. Yet that person must continue to live in the flesh until Christ returns or until death. Although holding citizenship in Heaven, we believers are still bound to Earth for a while longer, and we are expected to act as Christ's ambassadors until He returns for His people. I will try to cover the ways we can walk in the Spirit and attend to spiritual matters of God's Body while letting the new man inside our flesh walk in the physical realm displaying the fruits of our maturity.

God's Word gives us some instruction on how we are to relate to the world around us and how we are to make decisions. I trust that you will be made aware of and challenged by the Scriptures that will be covered. In Scripture God establishes boundaries, limits, penalties, and precepts that He expects to be adhered to in order for the believer to run the race and finish a winner, as did Paul. He also gave us tools of various types to use against our enemies, the dark forces of evil; unfortunately, many do not know which tool to use or how to use it or when to use it.

I am writing primarily for the benefit of people not called to ministry offices in the Body. The three areas of this chapter are as follows:

- Doing the works of Jesus
- Submission to authorities
- Walking in love

Believers who confess that they have matured spiritually should be incorporating all three of these important areas into their daily lives, or else they may not be positioned where they think in the Lord. If you truly desire the power of God to operate through you and dramatically touch the lives of people you contact, then you must not only commit to and act on these areas, but you must also make them as much a functional part of your daily life as breathing air. Then the proper channel or conduit is ready for the move of God.

Doing the Works of Jesus

By means of a scriptural background to launch this last chapter, look with me in Galatians 5:16–25, where Paul was helping the new converts in the Galatia region understand how to live and walk in the Spirit, regardless of what the Judaizers told them about obeying the law of Moses.

So I say, let the Holy Spirit guide your lives. Then you won't be doing what your sinful nature craves. The sinful nature wants to do evil, which is just the opposite of what the Spirit wants. And the Spirit gives us desires that are the opposite of what the sinful nature desires. These two forces are constantly fighting each other, so you are not free to carry out your good intentions. But when you are directed by the Spirit, you are not under obligation to the law of Moses. When you follow the desires of your sinful nature, the results are very clear: sexual immorality, impurity, lustful pleasures, idolatry, sorcery, hostility, quarreling, jealousy, outbursts of anger, selfish ambition, dissension, division, envy, drunkenness, wild parties, and other sins like these. Let me tell you again, as I have before, that anyone living that sort of life will not inherit the Kingdom of God. But the Holy Spirit produces this kind of fruit in our lives: love, joy, peace, patience, kindness, goodness, faithfulness, gentleness, and self-control. There is no law against these things! Those who belong to Christ Jesus have nailed the passions and desires of their sinful nature to his cross and crucified them there. Since we are living by the Spirit, let us follow the Spirit's leading in every part of our lives. (NLT)

These verses are very clear about the good fruits produced by believers following the leading of God's Spirit and how they contrast to the bad fruit produced outwardly by carnal Christians being led by their souls and bodies. It is a critical decision to make: am I going to walk in the Spirit or in the flesh, fulfilling carnal desires?

Choosing to walk in the flesh will not have been the right decision for believers found standing before Jesus at the Judgment Seat of Christ. As I have covered earlier, they will be standing on the left side with the other goats. Christ will judge their motives, their works, and the resulting fruit of those works, and they will be rewarded accordingly. It will be a fearful sight that all believers will witness. I trust that you will not be in that group of goats but that you will have chosen to walk in the Spirit and be both obedient and productive for the Kingdom.

It is important to understand that God has fully equipped the Spirit-filled believer with everything he needs to do the will of God on Earth. (Do you remember these words: *Thy will be done on Earth as it is in Heaven?*) Our purpose as believers on Earth is *to do whatever God has called us to do.* Some call this lay ministry; I call it the responsibility of every believer.

Each one of us is uniquely created and endowed by God with certain gifts, talents, and abilities that were placed within to accomplish His purposes, which vary somewhat from person to person. You must find out your purpose in life, or as some say, your calling in life. Your calling is not to attend church or partake in a Bible study group. It is not to live quietly in your neighborhood and be on the PTA committee at school. *Your commission, your calling, is to do the works of Jesus.*

We are His disciples, and He sends us forth into the world to minister in His name. He foretold that His Word and ministry in this world would be divisive, that He was the stone that the builders rejected but which became the chief cornerstone and is the same stone God uses for breaking people, grinding them to powder. He did His Father's work and fulfilled His divine mission on Earth several thousand years ago.

Some people don't seem to realize that when Jesus rose from the dead and sent the Holy Spirit, He had *completed* His ministry on Earth. On the cross He said, "It is finished." The keys to the Kingdom were handed over to His believers on Earth, to go forth and reap the harvest until He returned in the sky for them. He had planted all the necessary seeds and sent the Holy Spirit to water them.

The ongoing harvest is our job! The only remaining acts to be done by Him *on Earth* is to set up His millennial Kingdom in Jerusalem and rule for a thousand years after the tribulation period is past, soon after followed by the creation of a new Earth (and Heaven above it). The other events that are foretold involving Jesus will occur above the Earth or in Heaven itself. Again, Jesus completed His work *on* the Earth!

Let's take inventory on just what we have available by which to live and walk daily in the spirit realm, and see if there is anything lacking.

1. We're protected all around: a shield of faith, helmet of salvation, feet covered by the peace that comes through preparation in the Word of Truth, girdle of truth over loins, breastplate of righteousness for armor, and the sword of the Spirit (the Word of Truth and Life, Eph. 6:11, 13–17). Notice that there is no provision made for protection of the backside. Our battle dress is designed to be offensive for victory, not for retreat.

2. Our enemies are clearly identified for us.

> For we wrestle not against flesh and blood, but against principalities, against powers, against the rulers of

the darkness of this world, against spiritual wicked-
ness in high places.

Ephesians 6:12

(For though we walk in the flesh, we do not war
after the flesh: For the weapons of our warfare are
not carnal, but mighty through God to the pulling
down of strong holds:) Casting down imaginations,
and every high thing that exalteth itself against the
knowledge of God, and bringing into captivity every
thought to the obedience of Christ.

2 Corinthians 10:3–5

Demons gain access through the soul, first by thoughts
interjected directly into the mind and then by our entertaining
those thoughts as imaginations. As we imagine those things,
our emotions enter in and the body and its lusts are affected.
If we continue to dwell on that thing, we will open a door
for further imaginations along that same line and get weaker
in resistance. Soon a demonic stronghold is established, and
we come under direct demonic influence or addiction in that
area of life.

3. We have open, direct communications with our Father in
   Heaven at all times. He tells us, warns us, reveals to us,
   inspires us, and strengthens us through many channels:
   by His written Word (Jesus), His Spirit within us, dreams,
   visions, tongues with interpretation, and prophecy. Ephesians
   2:18 speaks of the accomplishment of Jesus on our behalves
   so that we do not have to go through human priests, clergy,
   prophets, or other men to talk directly to God in prayer:
   "For through him we both have access by one Spirit unto
   the Father." We can come boldly before God at His throne
   because we are high priests in Christ Jesus.

4. When we are uncertain about how to pray to our Father, His
   Spirit within us prays to Him *for us* and covers the subject

completely. We do not know what He says because it is in a language that is unknown to us.

In Ephesians 6:18–20, Paul requested of the churches in Galatia that they *pray in the Spirit* for him and for all the believers so that he would have supernatural utterance and be able to speak boldly on Scripture. Paul repeated Jesus' command to the believers in Ephesians 5:18: "Be filled with the Spirit." Paul stated to the church at Corinth: "For if I pray in an unknown tongue, my *spirit* prayeth.... I thank my God, I speak with tongues *more* than ye all" (1 Cor. 14: 4, 18, emphasis added).

5. We have the Holy Spirit within us, and He has an arsenal of powerful weapons at His disposal to operate through us when He decides to—the *gifts of the Spirit*. These spiritual gifts are described to us in 1 Corinthians 12:7–11 (emphasis added).

> But the manifestation of the Spirit is *given to every man* to profit withal. For to one is given by the Spirit the word of wisdom; to another the word of knowledge by the same Spirit; To another faith by the same Spirit; to another the gifts of healing by the same Spirit; To another the working of miracles; to another prophecy; to another discerning of spirits; to another divers kinds of tongues; to another the interpretation of tongues; But all these worketh that one and the selfsame Spirit, dividing to every man severally as he will.

6. We have spiritual authority and its resulting government in God's Church Body so that we can be effective in marching into battle together with others utilizing their gifts, talents, anointings, and abilities for the collective good. There are three good references to confirm the order, authority, and benefit of gifts that God has set in place.

And he gave some, apostles; and some, prophets; and some, evangelists; and some, pastors and teachers; For the perfecting of the saints, for the work of the ministry, for the edifying of the body of Christ: *Till we all come in the unity of the faith,* and of the knowledge of the Son of God, unto a perfect man, unto the measure of the stature of the fullness of Christ.

Ephesians 4:11–13, emphasis added

Now concerning spiritual gifts, brethren, I would not have you ignorant.... Now there are diversities of gifts, but the same Spirit. And there are differences of administrations, but the same Lord. And there are diversities of operations, but it is the same God which worketh all in all.

1 Corinthians 12:1, 4–6

And God hath set some in the church, first apostles, secondarily prophets, thirdly teachers, after that miracles, then gifts of healings, helps, governments, diversities of tongues.

1 Corinthians 12:28

7. We have faith to acquire or appropriate from the spirit realm what we have need of in the physical realm. Look with me at these three verses:

For your father knoweth what things ye have need of, before ye ask him.

Matthew 6: 8

But my God shall supply all your need according to his riches in glory by Christ Jesus.

Philippians 4:19

> We having the same spirit of faith, according as it is written, I *believed,* and therefore have I *spoken;* we also believe, and therefore speak.
>
> 2 Corinthians 4:13 (emphasis added)

8. We have the Word of Life and the Holy Spirit to lead us, to guide our steps, to build our faith, and to speak to us.

9. We can have, and should expect, supernatural *signs and wonders* to follow the preaching of God's Word of Life. These marvelous works of the Spirit will arrest people who do not know God and allow His Spirit to draw them to salvation. They will also increase faith in the believers who witness such moves of God in their midst and the resulting fruit.

10. Jesus has given, or delegated, to us authority and power over evil spirits, sickness, disease, and infirmity through God's decree. Our authority derives from our use of the *name of Jesus,* verbally and openly, and on faith in His Word.

> Then he called his twelve disciples together, and gave them *power and authority over all devils,* and *to cure diseases.* And he sent them to preach the Kingdom of God, and *to heal the sick.*
>
> Luke 9:1 (emphasis added)

> Which he wrought in Christ, when he raised him from the dead, and set him at his own right hand in the Heavenly places, Far above all principality, and power, and might, and dominion, and every name that is named, not only in this world, but also in that which is to come: And hath put all things under his feet, and gave him to be the head over all things to the church, Which is his body, the fullness of him that filleth all in all.
>
> Ephesians 1: 20–23

> And having spoiled principalities and powers, he made a shew of them openly, triumphing over them in it.
>
> Colossians 2:15

Jesus' perfect life as a man, His torment and bloody death as our sacrifice, and then His resurrection from the power of death (with Him as the firstfruits) qualified Him uniquely to take authority over all spiritual evil and its manifold works. He openly subjugated and humiliated the hierarchy of demon powers before all entities of the spirit realm, establishing forever His Lordship.

This list could be longer, but my point here is that God has provided for our lives, our needs, our victories, our bodies, and our futures. If we have been filled with His Spirit, feed on His Word as the daily Bread of Life, spend time before Him in prayer, die to self, and walk in faith, we have everything available to run the race to completion, to do our Father's will, and to produce good, lasting fruit from good works. Our rewards will be great, and we will dwell in the city of lights eternally.

The more we understand the awesome privileges available to us in Christ Jesus, the less puny and whiny about the cares and issues of this life we will be in our prayer lives, on our jobs, and before our families. We will live as men and women of integrity with character traits acquired from God that are consistent before the world. We must be givers and not takers, producers instead of consumers of resources.

As the Body of Christ, we need to stand up and begin talking and acting like all these things are available to us, that we are a powerful force for God's purposes upon the Earth, and that we have all the necessary means to overcome any obstacle in life. Let us lay down the vanities, pettiness (immaturity), and jealousies that abound within today's churches. Let's aim to get in sync, in agreement, with other believers around the world (instead of looking for their weaknesses) so that we can walk in lockstep in the Army of Christ, with the same uniformity and precision required of individuals marching at military academies. We must get our act together, or we will not be effective and profitable laborers in the fields that are now white unto harvest.

If this awareness and knowledge of who we are in Christ Jesus becomes our mind-set, we will need very little supernatural intervention by the Holy Spirit or angels on our behalves while we accomplish His will on Earth. Our needs will be mostly for guidance (Spirit-led) and for protection (spiritual warfare).

We will always be dependent upon the Holy Spirit for His anointing, His operation of spiritual gifts, and other things of the spirit realm that I have touched on. Those things are accomplished at His will, as the Father instructs Him, and in His time. What I am referring to as our walk in the Spirit as mature believers are those areas that are at *our* initiative, at *our* request, and in *our* desired time frame. The more that we walk in the Spirit daily, the more synchronous we will become in thought and time with the Holy Spirit, and the more equipped we'll be to get the job done without continuous hand-holding from Him.

Think of the raising of children: You begin their training, and they learn a step at a time—how to walk, how to talk, how to act within and without the family unit, how to begin making their own simple decisions—leading right up to as much practical independence as feasible. With proper training (discipleship, Bible study, prayer), life experience, and time, believers should be progressing through developmental stages of spiritual growth and discipline to the point of being able to take care of many things on their own with the provisions given by our Lord.

We can see this in the Gospels: how Jesus taught and trained the disciples in learning to handle the spiritual provisions made available to them. Then He sent them out to practice and refine what He had placed within them. When they were considered ready for more mature spiritual-life challenges, He sent them out as apostles to start churches and to disciple other people, who would disciple others, who would disciple others, in perpetuity. They were trained and equipped just like soldiers; then they received their commissions and went forth to battle. The "general" still looked down on their progress, directed their strategy at a high level, and sent in reinforcements when needed.

When an army recruit reports to boot camp, he is excited about learning the army way of life: self-discipline, educational training, physical fitness, submission to authority, weapon training, and so forth. We are the same way when we enter the Kingdom of God. We study the Word, sit under great teaching, learn the weapons and objects of our warfare, understand the concept of submission to authority, and get ourselves spiritually fit.

Now what do we do with all that training and education? Most believers do very little or nothing with it. They do not have a proper vision of their roles in the Army of God. They ignore their commission and do not ship out for active duty in combat situations around the globe. Instead, they sit comfortably in church and squander the time and resources poured into them during their training. It is getting to be a late hour on the world's time clock, and we must labor before it is dark and no one can labor. We must start mobilizing ourselves and go do what we have been called and trained to do!

Today's local churches and ministry organizations have in some ways deviated from Jesus' plan. Yes, we do have some men and women of God discipling others, training them in spiritual matters, getting them equipped for warfare, and sending them out into the world as salt and light. However, those are in *the minority*. Instead, most churches are focused on keeping the current members happy, gaining a few new members each year, getting a few people saved at the altars, and keeping a progressive image or modern profile within the community—*not* on equipping the saints for warfare and sending them out into the world. Most ministries today show the following patterns that reflect the spiritual condition of the church:

- Ministry name is that of the founder. *Whose* ministry is it, anyway?

- Ministry events (conferences, revivals, camp meetings, and other such events) are focused in name and promotion upon the higher-profile, "successful" minister(s) attending.

- There is little power of the Spirit present in the services—
healings, deliverance from demonic oppression and possession, operation of the gifts of the Spirit, signs and wonders
following the preaching of God's Word.

- Most attendees are already followers of the ministry or
minister. Most are in attendance to get fatter spiritually on
the Word and are given no challenge to start acting on their
faith with good works, to pray and fast throughout the event,
to bring in the lost from the highways and hedges, to carry in
the lame, and to go to the hospitals and prisons. Why aren't
the lost drawn into these services by word-of-mouth testi-
monies they hear in stores, schools, and businesses about the
glory of God being manifested in the meetings?

- Even mature attendees do not usually bring the lost, sick,
demonized, deformed, and crippled into the meetings. Even if
they do, there still may not be ministry to those specific needs
during or after the service, thus creating disappointment.

- There is usually a significant fee required for the event,
bought in advance, just like for secular events.

- In addition to the event fee, there may be a focus placed on
further giving to the ministry during the event, usually for a
"special need" of some sort.

- The ministers who speak are usually not accessible to the
audience, even to shake hands after the service. It is an imper-
sonal ministry from the stage, all tightly choreographed and
moved along according to a prescribed time line. Nothing,
even the operation of spiritual gifts within or among the
body, is allowed to interfere with the prescribed sequence of
planned steps by the worship leader and minister, ultimately
leading to an altar call at the end. Yes, reaching a time of decision to commit to God is the goal of most public ministry,
but the Holy Spirit must be the one who determines when

and how that point is reached, when hearts are prepared to receive Him.

- There is usually a push made during the service or event for the purchase of speakers' CDs, DVDs, books, event T-shirts, paperweights, and other merchandise, which is prominently displayed close by. Does this promotion of merchandise have to be done from the stage?

- The ministry is eventually handed down to the son of the founder, whether or not he is called and chosen for that office or anointed for that ministry. This is simply presumption on the part of the ministry family unless God has clearly indicated already that this is His divine plan for the church or ministry team.

    You can judge the fruits of these ministries and know if their inheriting the ministry from Papa was God's plan or not. God may have been developing and grooming an anointed, nonfamily minister to take over that responsibility. Again, *whose* ministry is it, anyway? It doesn't (or shouldn't) belong to the founding family—it is God's!

- The ministry that achieves some success (fame, privilege, wealth, prosperity) usually becomes smitten with its success and wants to grow and expand. This necessitates hiring staff, hiring various consultants, expanding office space and building new complexes, buying time on radio, and producing television programs. These changes then require more money to operate the ministry, and thus begins a continuous, steep climb up the slippery slope of fundraising projects that consume time, dilute available resources, and can quench the Spirit of God's anointing upon that ministry or minister. Large organizations lead to large staffs and large budgets that have to be maintained. Some of the staff may be dedicated entirely to fundraising projects and promotional displays, not to ministry.

God does intend to grow His Kingdom into all the world, exponentially, but I see in Scripture where that growth is accomplished more in disciple-by-disciple, house-to-house, cell-group-by-cell-group, and church-by-church ministry instead of a few gigantic ministries with huge overhead expenses. (I am not including evangelists in this point. My concern is expressed mainly to pastors and apostles who may give more energy to building their ministries and influence than to building the Kingdom of God.) My study of Scripture leads me to the conclusion that God would rather have twenty thousand trained and equipped points of His light dispersed into the world than to have twenty thousand members sitting in a megachurch getting fat on the Bread of Life.

- A ministry considered successful is expected to reflect prosperity in many ways— in clothing, modes of transportation when traveling, residences, personal automobiles, private schools or tutors for the kids, club memberships, special honors, and so forth. Not too many years ago, these were the same milestones of success by which the world judged Hollywood celebrities and industrial barons.

- Gimmicks begin to appear in the ministry: special offers made to gain financial partners; merchandise given away to get new donors; specialists arising in certain areas of Bible teaching; sales made of various oils, handkerchiefs, waters, nutritional supplements, and faith-helpers; experts brought in to motivate, mentor, teach, or engineer special effects, do comedy routines, write books from the compilation of messages and teachings, or prepare cute audiovisual presentations; and many other distractions from true spiritual ministry. It seems that many of today's ministers feel that the work of the Holy Spirit alone is not adequate to draw sufficient numbers to finance the burgeoning operational budget.

- Discipleship of new converts is almost unheard of in today's churches and ministries. Ministers should be imitating Christ: *making* new converts, *discipling* them, *establishing* them in the Word, *directing* them to get some personal ministry experience under their belts, and then *releasing them* into the world! This is God's established pattern for changing cities, states, provinces, and nations. How else will His Body disciple nations? Why is this proven pattern prescribed by Jesus not being replicated throughout the Body of Christ, particularly by those standing in ministry offices?

These issues are identified here not to criticize, but to show areas, even in ministry organizations, where the works of Jesus are not so evident because of a scarcity of evident fruit. What needs to change to properly *mobilize* the body for service? Is merely being *equipped* for service enough to fulfill our Great Commission and bring glory to the Father? Let us now challenge ourselves, our submission to and our maturity in Christ Jesus, by holding up the standards described in the New Testament for believers and see how we fare against them.

We need to act more than we talk. Our works need to be developing so they will bear good fruit in season. We must be disciplined people, getting our flesh under submission to our spirits and renewed souls, and placing ourselves under submission to those in spiritual authority over us. Either we believe and act on what Jesus said, or we leave it to everyone else to do the works of Jesus on the Earth.

Here are a few examples of the situations in which the mature believer can act on what is available to him or to her.

1. A friend becomes sick and requests prayer. Response: *You* go pray for your friend's healing. Jesus has already paid the price for the person's healing. The Word gives faith to the sick to believe it and receive healing. You pray the prayer of faith for your friend's healing. Take someone with you to pray the prayer of agreement. As an additional aid, take anointing oil and anoint the person when praying for his healing. If available, take along someone who has the Holy Spirit operating

gifts of healing through him or her, with prior fruit borne of their healing ministry.

Yes, lift the sick person up in prayer to God, but realize that God's Son has already come from Heaven and taken care of healing on Earth. He expects you and me to do the work with what He's given us already. The pastor doesn't have to be the one to visit the sick for their healing—*you* can!

This type of action is not limited to being a ministerial function, no matter what your dead church has convinced you through years of inactivity and traditional teaching with no works put to faith. Do you have faith in God's Word or not? It clearly tells us what has been done and what things we are supposed to do. His Word tells us what we can expect by stepping out to do the works that Jesus did, in love and faith and power, for our fellow man.

2. A person is bothered, oppressed, or addicted. He asks for help, wanting deliverance and healing. We call upon God in prayer to deliver him from his pain, torment, or compulsion.

   Now what? Do you call the pastor and ask him to pray for or visit the person, then sit back and hope for good news? You might, but *you* can go and pray the prayer of deliverance and healing. You have been given the authority over all devils of hell; you have the authority to speak in Jesus' name to spirits and causative agents; and you have the Word of Truth to stand on, declaring all of this as truth. Jesus is sitting on His throne beside the Father and is not coming back down to repeat what He has already finished. He gave to *us*, His Body of believers, the keys to the Kingdom! Let's go open some doors and make things happen for God's glory.

3. Someone has a need: a job, a way to get to work, someone to babysit a toddler while he or she works, groceries for the week, and so forth. Who's going to supply the needs? Jesus is not coming down from Heaven to do it. The Holy Spirit can work behind the scenes to open doors of opportunity, to set up situations, or to grant favor with man, but who makes

the supply arrive? Answer: the Body of Christ, believers who realize that cars and babysitters don't just fall out of the sky and that Jesus is not going to show up for chauffeur duty.

The early Church came together in unity and in love, allowing for everyone's needs to be met. The Body of Christ on Earth is Jesus' feet, hands, and head today. *We do the work,* and His unseen hand works behind the scenes *to help us* as His Spirit *leads us.* Jesus orchestrates the ministry from Heaven through His Holy Spirit in us. We do the work, our good works bear good fruit, and the Father receives glory— all because of the tremendous sacrifice that Jesus made for mankind.

When our Lord hung on the cross and was about to expire, He stated that His work on Earth was *finished.* We believers need to recognize this fact and move on in our responsibilities to one another and to the dark world of sinners. Soon it will be night when no one can work in the fields to harvest the crop.

John 9:4–5 should give us the perspective we need in today's world: "I must work the works of him that sent me, while it is day: the night cometh, when no man can work. As long as I am in the world, I am the light of the world." Today's believers have assumed those two roles, among many, since the resurrection and ascension into Heaven of Jesus: doing the *works* that we are called to do (that will glorify the Father) and being the *light* (and salt) of the world. Jesus is no longer *in* the world, and we are His agents, His ambassadors, to accomplish His purposes.

A word about ambassadors is in order since that role has been delegated to us by our Lord. Look at Paul's writing to the church at Ephesus in Ephesians 6:19–20: "And for me, that utterance may be given unto me, that I may open my mouth boldly, to make known the mystery of the gospel, For which I am an ambassador in bonds: that therein I may speak boldly, as I ought to speak." Paul understood that he was Christ's ambassador and that his role should allow him to speak boldly concerning the gospel message. He knew that being an ambassador was a serious role for anyone.

- An ambassador is appointed. It is not an elected or inherited position. A person cannot appoint himself to this position. (This is analogous to an anointing.)

- An ambassador is appointed by the highest authority in government, as our President appoints ambassadors to represent our nation overseas. (Jesus commissioned us.)

- An ambassador talks and acts directly on behalf of the one who appointed him. (We are ambassadors on Earth for Christ and His Heavenly Kingdom.)

- An ambassador receives privileges and access that are not available to most others. (We are a royal priesthood that can enter boldly into the throne room, and we are given gifts and operations of the Holy Spirit.)

- An ambassador's position is an official one, with a proper procedure required to be followed for the person to become official in his duties. (We must be born again of the Spirit and of water to become children of God.)

- An ambassador receives credentials that show his position and source of authority to act in an official capacity. (We are given authority over all evil spirits, we are given the name of Jesus to use, we have been given the Word of Life and Truth, and we have been given His Spirit to dwell within us.)

Without further elaboration, know that we believers are Christ's ambassadors and that we represent Him across the Earth—to kings all the way down to the poorest person. We talk and act for Him (works), and we are credentialed in an official capacity. We are His light in a world of darkness. Only we believers are qualified and able to bring the good news of salvation to those bound in chains.

Are we doing this mission for Him, or are we sitting idle in a pew or maybe giving a warmed-over message on stage at some event made more interesting by the use of some slick props for illustration?

We know that America has gradually slid into a mire of sin, as the Hebrew nation in Israel did so many times, and has influenced many other nations in atheism, greed, corporate corruption, burdensome and even petty lawsuits, witchcraft, and other unrighteous practices. Is judgment coming? Are there intercessors on their knees calling out to God for mercy, for grace, for long-suffering, for patience, and for the salvation of our great nation? How is the United States of America to be saved from judgment? Who is going to do it?

Neither Jesus nor the Holy Spirit is going to evangelize our nation. Don't say others will do it, because it is too big of a job for a few. It is *you and I* who must get up, shake off all the weak excuses for our inaction, break off the shell of complacency that has grown over us, and go out as lights into darkness.

All believers must realize that *they* are the ones to do the works of Jesus in our land. We have been fully equipped, have been delegated full authority over our enemies, and have the Holy Spirit within us to take us to the battle's front lines. If we are ashamed, timid, shy, unwilling, unprepared, ill-equipped, or not fit, then we are still consumers in the Body and not ready for duty as mature men and women of God.

Yes, there will be some casualties. You didn't conveniently read over those Scriptures about martyrs, traps, snares, deceivers, seducers, beheadings, trials, sufferings, and tribulations of the righteous, did you? Some of us may pay a great price for our good works, but we should be like Paul and *count it joy* to do the works that we are called by God to do. In Heaven the price will seem insignificant compared to the rewards gained! *We* must mobilize believers across the globe and get about the Father's business while we can. There is no one else to accomplish the work.

There are two more subject areas that I want to comment on as we near the end of this book: submission to authority and love. I have found that most Christians who are unbalanced, inactive/idle/uninvolved, contentious, rebellious (unruly), insincere, proud, or who fail in their obedience to Christ's commandments are very weak in one or both of these areas. Let's look at each of them separately and then step back and look at the force of the two in combination with the works of Jesus in a believer's life.

Submission to Authority

All creation has established order that God instituted for our protection. In God's Kingdom of Heaven, there are orders of angels: angelic levels of lower authority (cherubim, for example) and of higher authority (archangels) identified in Scripture. There is a hierarchy of evil spirits (demons) under Satan's rule.

Mankind has multiple levels of governmental authority on Earth, and Jesus tells us in the Word of Truth that God raises up and establishes the rulers, whether good or bad, for His purposes. Pilate was shocked when Jesus pointed that irony out to him when Pilate was questioning His authority and His Kingdom on Earth (John 19:10–11.)

Many people just can't accept that God places people in positions of authority—the President of the United States, governors, judges, sheriffs—because they see some who are corrupt, incompetent, or unstable in their ways. However, remember that God placed just the right son of the royal family in position as Pharaoh before Joseph arrived in Egypt. He later placed another man in the same lineage, who was mean, evil, hard-hearted and who worshipped other deities, in power as Pharaoh before the return to Egypt of Moses with Aaron. These people were pawns of God in His great plans for His people. He used them to get glory among the nations and to preserve His chosen people. He doesn't do any less for Himself or His people in today's world.

There would be chaos in all of creation without order, and the order of each realm is maintained by the levels of authority. Christians have authorities and order established within the Body of Christ for their good or profit: marriage, family, church, and ministry. Many like to think of themselves as free as birds once they are saved, but salvation is merely the beginning point, like entering boot camp in the military. This is one reason that there are references to believers being in the Army of God. It is not just mental and physical preparation, weapons of warfare, fitness level, and motivation—it is recognizing that you are now under many levels of authority, that you must learn to recognize those in authority (rank), and that you are going to be given orders throughout your career in the army.

How would the army march men around the parade grounds if they did not know whose orders to follow or be willing to follow them? How would the officers line up the men and keep the lines straight if not for the discipline that authority establishes within the ranks? If you are responsible and obedient in taking orders and fulfilling assignments, you may have men placed under *your* authority. You will be promoted in rank and rise in level of authority the more submitted, obedient, effective, and faithful you prove to be.

Folks, this is what enlisting in the Army of God involves. You are not free to come and go where and when you please, moving around churches, picking and choosing how much you give of yourself, or deciding whether you volunteer to help. You come under the God-established authority of spiritual men and women in the Body of Christ, and it is of paramount importance that you submit to this authority. Otherwise, you will be like a ship without both a rudder and an anchor. Young Christians often have a difficult time understanding authority in the Body of Christ when they have not been discipled by their parents, but it is there and has to be recognized through Bible study, effectual prayer, and the Holy Spirit's enlightenment.

Seek God for your place to plug in and settle down to do the work that He has called you to do! Find a minister under whom you can submit yourself for instruction, rebuke, and spiritual growth. Otherwise, you will not find contentment, and you will not do good works and bear good fruit for the Kingdom. I speak from experience on that point. Ministers need to submit themselves to a senior minister or to a group of independent ministers under whom they can receive spiritual oversight, receive guidance in major decision-making, receive correction and righteous rebuke (if and when needed), bounce ideas off of, and receive discipleship in areas of weakness or inexperience.

Let's look at some key Scriptures that speak to issues and principles of authority, submission, and obedience in the Body of Christ so that we can learn from them, apply them to our lives, and let God's Spirit loose us for greater good works and resulting good fruit. The Body of Christ has to learn submission to ordained authorities, or else it will be weak and unfocused, without leadership within the members.

Exodus 18:21–22 reads: "Moreover thou shalt provide out of all the people able men, such as fear God, men of truth, hating covetousness; and place such over them, to be rulers of thousands, and rulers of hundreds, rulers of fifties, and rulers of tens: And let them judge the people at all seasons." This Scriptural passage is most often recited solely in the context of Moses being advised that he needed help governing the Hebrew nation on their extended trek toward Canaan. However, this is a clear example of God's earliest order, or hierarchy, of leadership being installed in the ranks of His people for governance. Men were placed both over some people and under other people for the purpose of having lines of authority established.

Look at the qualifications of these men who were to be selected for bearing this responsibility: spiritually fit (able), accountable (fearing God), truthful, and not the least inclined to desire others' property. This new governmental structure with men of integrity in leadership brought ministry, protection, and supply into a much more efficient structure in the camp than just one man leading all and bearing the burdens of all.

In like manner Jesus delegated spiritual authority over evil spirits to His disciples (us believers) on Earth but also established godly order by setting overseers/apostles, shepherds, elders, deacons, bishops, prophets, administrations, and so forth throughout His Kingdom for there to be lines of authority and more efficient ministry, protection, and supply. Any form of authority, secular or spiritual, is only as strong as its structural integrity and the submission to it by its members.

Hebrews 13:7, 17, 34 says: "Remember *them which have the rule over you,* who have spoken unto you the word of God: whose faith follow, considering the end of their conversation.... Obey *them that have the rule over you,* and *submit yourselves:* for they watch for your souls, as they that must give account, that they may do it with joy, and not with grief: for that is unprofitable for you.... Salute all *them that have the rule over you,* and all the saints" (emphasis added). Paul understood authority, both spiritual and secular types.

He understood that authority was God's source of maintaining order and getting work done.

These positions of authority are God-given and are the result of faithfulness and good stewardship. We are to follow their teachings and obey their instructions. It is for our good that He places men and women in spiritual authority in the Body. Paul knew that those in authority would be held accountable to God for their steward-ship and care of those under them. He knew that your submission to designated authority was profitable for the Kingdom and that rebel-lion would grieve those over you and hinder growth (fruit), resulting in *your* being held accountable for your rebellion and the problems it caused for others.

Matthew 8:7–10, 13 is one of my favorite passages to enlighten believers about authority and submission, which most people are resistant to accept since it sounds controlling on the surface. However, *problems (rebellion)* submitting to authority began in Heaven with Lucifer, continued down on Earth in Eden, and have followed a steady course throughout man's history, both in the secular world and in God's Kingdom on Earth. Here is the response by Jesus when confronted by a rare man who was a believer and who also under-stood authority.

> And Jesus saith unto him, I will come and heal him. The centurion answered and said, Lord, I am not worthy that thou shouldest come under my roof: but speak the word only, and my servant shall be healed. For I am a man under authority, having soldiers under me: and I say to this man, Go, and he goeth; and to another, Come, and he cometh; and to my servant, Do this, and he doeth it. When Jesus heard it, he marvelled, and said to them that followed, Verily I say unto you, I have not found so great faith, no, not in Israel.... And Jesus said unto the centurion, Go thy way; as thou hast believed, so be it done unto thee. And his servant was healed in the selfsame hour.

Please get the principles of this passage deep into your spirit, for they will open up much growth and spiritual development, making your walk in the Spirit much more effective and with less time required to achieve results.

- The centurion *acknowledged* his unworthiness before the Lamb of God. As a believer, he could have acted like I've seen and heard people of God do in church: pushing and shoving to get to the speaker, demanding that the minister come and pray for their loved ones, reminding the minister of who they are in the church (gifts and tithes, seniority, status). This man, who was an important officer in the hated Roman army, came in humility (not by force), for he was a servant and he recognized his Master.

- The centurion was seeking healing from Jesus for his servant *out of love* for the person. How many men of stature, even in this day, would go to this trouble for a servant? The man had compassion on his tormented servant back at the house and was seeking permanent, complete relief from Jesus, the source of life.

- The man recognized the absolute authority of Jesus and knew that there was no need for Him to come physically to pray for his tormented servant.

- The man had already learned what authority involves; he *told* Jesus that and gave several examples to confirm his clear understanding. He was both under the authority of others, and he was in authority over others. Here was a soldier who lived with order and authority structures in the army; yet he knew that a parallel structure of authority existed in the Kingdom of Heaven and that Jesus was at the top of the order!

- By the centurion's knowledge and submission to authority (power), he knew and *stated* to Jesus that it was only the *spoken* word of Jesus (*rhema*) that needed to be *heard* for the thing to be done in another city. His faith was in Jesus as the head of all authority and power, and his *spoken* faith and understanding of these principles was unusual for this time and place, particularly for a Gentile.

• Jesus marveled at the man's comprehension of these critical principles and his bold, *outspoken* declaration of faith in Jesus' spoken word. Jesus turned and announced to His followers that He had not found anyone in Israel with as much faith as this man. (Notice the words I've put in italics that emphasize the importance of the spoken word for faith to be operated and for it to acquire things in the spirit realm and bring them into the physical realm. Faith requires love and the human voice to be actuated in the physical realm.) For Jesus to marvel, He was impressed to see the fruit of His ministry so clearly on display in this centurion's life. At times Jesus had problems getting His own chosen disciples to grasp the teachings, both public and private, that He gave on the principles of authority in the Kingdom of God (see Matt. 20:20–28).

• Now for the essence of this passage as it applies to us readers: Jesus stated that *as the centurion believed, so it would be done*. This soldier had compassion for his servant, had faith in the source of healing, and understood the principle of authority. He confessed before the crowd his trust in Jesus as the apex of all authority and acknowledged that Jesus only had to say a word of healing for it to be done.

This is where we have to search our hearts and question whether our ultimate motive is love, whether we speak and act in faith, whether we understand the authority structure ordained by God in His Church Body, and whether we willingly submit to that structure now that Jesus is no longer here on Earth. Let us be mature men and women of God and not whiny babies. May we go into the world and boldly minister to others (producers) instead of constantly needing something from our church and fellow believers (consumers).

Mark 13:34 gives us a picture of Jesus' delegation of authority to His believers in His Church Body: "For the Son of man is as a man taking a far journey, who left his house, and *gave authority to his servants, and to every man his work,* and commanded the porter to watch" (emphasis added). This passage refers to the spiritual authority instituted within the Body of Christ on Earth and the placing of our individual gifts, talents, and callings throughout His Body. Notice what follows in sequence once that authority structure is in place: each believer's calling. You cannot achieve your calling in this life outside of God's authority structure within His Body. Many people never find their callings because they are in rebellion against God's institution of government in His Church.

Please read Matthew 20:20–28 and 23:10–12 to understand the twin foundations of this God-ordained authority structure: servant-hood and humility. Jesus is our example at extreme ends of the spectrum of spiritual power, both at the apex of authority in the Church (Master) and in the lowly position of the greatest, most humble servant of all mankind. Built on these two foundation stones are stewardship, integrity, responsibility, faithfulness, wisdom, discretion, obedience, and other qualities that are evident (fruit-bearing) in mature believers promoted by God into positions of authority. These positions are not limited to those in ministry offices, although their burdens of responsibility are usually greater because of the number of people under their spheres of influence in public ministry.

For those who may question the believer's commission and role in the harvest of today's world of spiritual darkness, disease, infirmity, demon oppression, and spiritual warfare, let us understand what Jesus did when He felt that His work in preparing and equipping disciples was nearing completion. The following two verses are major in revealing to us the plan of Jesus to bring salvation to all mankind throughout the world when He would no longer be among us on Earth. Also, He did not do and say these things just to His own personally trained disciples, as some mistakenly teach, but established this enduring work for all believers for the ages to come. These disciples were the first to walk in this new level of ministry and are our examples to follow. As awesome as these responsibilities are for His commissioned believers, keep in mind that the disciples in these verses had not yet received the *fullness and power* of God's Spirit in the baptism of the Holy Ghost, which they later received on the Day of Pentecost.

Luke 9:1–2: "Then he called his twelve disciples together, and gave them power and authority over all devils, and to cure diseases. And he sent them to preach the Kingdom of God, and to heal the sick." This passage has to be one the most "rules-changing" precedents of all ages, forever changing the structures and accountability for God's ministry to the world. You can see here that Jesus delegated His spiritual authority to the disciples, and He sent them out to minister in that authority to the dying world. He did not say, Pray for them and I'll heal them, or Pray for them and I'll cast out demon spirits from them. No, He said for *them* to go out as His ambassadors and begin doing what they had seen Him doing. They were now fully equipped as believers to do that!

Look at what Jesus gave to His faithful believers: power and authority over evil spirits, diseases, and forms of sickness, as well as the calling or commission to preach the Kingdom of God to the entire world. This "wholesale change" that Jesus instituted meant that no longer were the king, the prophet, and the high priest the only ones anointed to minister in the name of God. He made *all believers* in Jesus, both Jew and Gentile, to be a nation of priests and kings unto God! (Revelation 1:6).

It is critically important that each of us realize here that we are part of a priesthood of believers, that we have been declared (and expected to be) a holy nation. We must be trained (discipled) and equipped for service then go out into the world and do the works of Jesus, being salt and light, fully empowered to do battle right in the enemy's territory—sickness, disease, infirmity, oppression, possession, witchcraft, and other kinds of demonic activities.

Most people and church denominations will accept the part about believers preaching the Kingdom of God, although they limit the scope of their understanding of that work to only those that are "called" to it, but they balk at *doing* the other works of Jesus, the ones that are not as easy, the ones that put believers on the front line of battle against the works of the enemy. It is much safer to sit back and feel content to financially support others through church outreach ministries (missions, street ministry, hospital visitation, and so forth) who are willing to go and to do for our God. However, that was not the plan that Jesus established on Earth prior to His departure. It is His plan for all believers to do His works within their spheres of influence and wherever else He may lead them to go.

One obvious and serious problem in believers doing the same works as Jesus is that there are so few people actually doing these works and training others in them. That is part of the discipling process: teaching the fundamentals in Scripture and practicing what you've learned. Unfortunately, few believers have been adequately taught the Word of Truth and even fewer have been shown, *by example,* how to heal the sick and deal with demonic manifestations.

To be a discipler of men requires a dedicated life and a commitment to holiness, love, servanthood, regular Bible study, a fervent desire and hunger for spiritual things, an active prayer life, being filled with God's Spirit, fasting, submission to spiritual and secular authority, and the other basics of becoming a mature and responsible Christian. Our churches and ministries need to develop a new strategy for their continued existence: train, equip, and disciple members in doing the works of Jesus and then release them to go into all the world. If they successfully do this, God's Spirit will bless and enlarge them beyond their wildest dreams.

Growth in membership itself is not the goal of the local church; it is to prepare workers for the great harvest throughout the world—from their backyards, to their neighborhoods, into the workplace, and into the rest of humanity. The people sitting in the pews from Sunday to Sunday are disciples in the process of training to become effective workers in the field. Anything less than that vision is merely show, delusion, or unfaithful stewardship of resources.

Paul, the most prolific of the New Testament authors, wrote many significant things regarding authority in the Church of God, our submission to it, and proper spiritual rule over others in his letters to the churches and leaders/co-leaders within his apostleship. Keep in mind that Paul was addressing these instructions also to believers in the churches, many of whom were supposedly mature believers. Let's take to heart his instructions.

1. To the church at Corinth: 1 Corinthians 16:15–16; 2 Corinthians 10:13, 15 (emphasis added)

> I beseech you, brethren, (ye know the house of Stephanas, that is the firstfruits of Achaia, and that they have addicted themselves to the ministry of the saints,) That ye *submit yourselves unto such*, and to every one that helpeth with us, and laboreth.... But we will not boast of things without our measure, but *according to the measure of the rule which God hath distributed to us,* a measure to reach even unto you.... Not boasting of things without our measure, that is, of other men's labours; but having hope, when your faith is increased, that we shall be enlarged by you *according to our rule* abundantly.

The authority structure was there and is here now. Paul was not going to boast about things done outside of his area of authority or by others who labored, only those things accomplished within the boundaries of his God-given work. Paul wanted the believers' faith to grow so that his area of work (and authority) for the Kingdom would be extended.

2. To the church at Rome: Romans 1:30; 12:8; 13:3–5 (emphasis added)

> Backbiters, haters of God, despiteful, proud, boasters, inventors of evil things, *disobedient to parents*.... Or he that exhorteth, on exhortation: he that giveth, let him do it with simplicity; *he that ruleth,* with diligence; he that sheweth mercy, with cheerfulness.... For *rulers* are not a terror to good works, but to the evil. Wilt thou then not be afraid of the *power?* Do that which is good, and thou shalt have praise of the same: For *he is the minister of God* to thee for good. But if thou do that which is evil, be afraid; for he beareth not the sword in vain: for *he is the minister*

of God, a revenger to execute wrath upon him that doeth evil. Wherefore *ye must needs be subject,* not only for wrath, but also for conscience sake.

Persons who are disobedient to their parents are unruly, defiant, and resistant to submitting to their parental and spiritual authorities. They disqualify themselves from serving in the Body. Look at the associated company they keep in Paul's list.

Disobedience is rebellion, which is a demonic spirit whose power has to be broken in a person's life before he can do good works or bear good fruit for the Kingdom. Unfortunately, I have witnessed several instances of grown men and women speaking disrespectfully to their parents or ignoring their counsel. None of them were producing fruit in the Body, although they may have held positions of authority in their local churches.

Paul's writings also equate rulers in the Body of Christ with ministers of God. These men and women may not be standing in a ministerial office but are still ministers to the Body whom God uses through their works, their influence, and their God-given authority to speak into people's lives. We must be subject to their authority and take their words and works seriously for our own benefit in the Body. Are you open and yielded to designated spiritual authority in the Body of Christ?

3. To the church at Ephesus: Ephesians 2:2; 5:6, 21 (emphasis added)

Wherein in time past ye walked according to the course of this world, according to the prince of the power of the air, the spirit that now worketh in *the children of disobedience....* Let no man deceive you with vain words: for because of these things cometh the wrath of God upon *the children of disobedi-*

ence.... Submitting yourselves one to another in the fear of God.

For the most part, these passages are self-explanatory. Note the strong linkage here between disobedience and the power of Satan over people, bringing the resulting wrath of God on them. To avoid that fate, we are to submit ourselves to one another in the Body, fearing the wrath of God if we remain disobedient.

God uses men and women in His Body to help His children achieve their purposes, their callings, in this life. Recognize that fact as the basis for the severity of punishment for disobedient children. We are disobedient to our Father when we refuse to submit to those He has placed over us in His government. It is a simple concept but one that is widely untaught in the modern church world. It is much, much easier to preach and teach prosperity and blessing than submission, serving, and humility.

If today's ministers will not teach all the principles of Kingdom living, God will raise up and promote others who will. Otherwise, His plan for man will not be attained because His Bride will not yet be prepared, His Army cannot march in step, and His Body is lacking all of its members, or parts. Remember, we cannot all be heads or hearts or lungs in the body. Some of us are to be toes, vertebrae, and toenails.

4. To the church at Thessalonica: 1 Thessalonians 5:12–14 (emphasis added)

> And we beseech you, brethren, to *know them which* labour among you, and *are over you in the Lord,* and admonish you; And to *esteem them very highly in love* for their work's sake. And be at peace among yourselves. Now we exhort you, brethren, *warn them that are unruly,* comfort the feebleminded, support the weak, be patient toward all men.

In these verses we get to see honoring, serving, admonishing, esteeming, ruling, submission, doing good works, and warning all neatly bundled together in a spiritual package. Paul says to get to know and to learn from those in spiritual authority who work among the church members. He goes much further by saying that those in authority should be highly esteemed by the showing of love by the church members.

How do you highly esteem such people by demonstrating your love for them and their beneficial works in the church? Most people don't know the available options because this is not being taught in today's churches. There is a variety of practical ways to show esteem; for example, by honoring, serving, and giving. These were taught to me, in love and with much patience, by a life-changing ministry of discipleship years ago. The principles have never left me; the opportunities to highly esteem fruitful ministers of God (both lay ministers in authority and pastoral staff holding office) have been few. This is an important subject area, but not for this book.

5. To the church at Colossae: Colossians 3:5–6 (emphasis added)

> Mortify therefore your members which are upon the earth; fornication, uncleanness, inordinate affection, evil concupiscence, and covetousness, which is idolatry: For which things' sake the wrath of God cometh on *the children of disobedience.*

Paul had preached to this church about seeking after and setting their affections upon spiritual things above. He had just reminded them that Christ Jesus was their life and they would see Him in glory. However, there was some spiritual housecleaning to do before the members got all misty-eyed thinking about Heaven; many of them were still carnal, and they were referred to as the children of disobedience. Why?

Because they had refused to submit themselves to the teachings of Jesus (the Word of Truth), to the Holy Spirit's conviction, and to the *overseers* of God's flock set by His Spirit in the local church for their good. All of these overseers had spoken in unity of the Spirit and had encouraged, counseled, and warned them about continuing in their carnal ways.

Paul calls their disobedience for what it is and states that they are inviting the wrath of God by their continued works of the flesh. These members had obviously ignored the examples set by those in authority, had refused their counsel and attempts at personal ministry, and had chosen (by not transforming their minds and getting their flesh under control) to go on their own course. They squandered all available resources and were bound to pay a heavy price for their sin.

6. To Timothy: 1 Timothy 1:9; 2:1–2; 3:4–5, 12; 5:17; 2 Timothy 3:2 (emphasis added)

> Knowing this, that the law is not made for a righteous man, but for *the lawless and disobedient,* for the ungodly, and for sinners, for unholy and profane, for *murderers of fathers and murderers of mothers,* for manslayers.... I exhort therefore, that, first of all, supplications, prayers, intercessions, and giving of thanks, be made for all men; *For kings, and for all that are in authority;* that we may lead a quiet and peaceable life in all godliness and honesty.... [Bishops:] *One that ruleth* his own house, having his children *in subjection* with all gravity; (For if a man know not *how to rule* his own house, how shall he *take care of* the church of God?).... Let the *deacons* be the husbands of one wife, *ruling* their children and their own houses well.... Let the *elders* that *rule well* be counted worthy of double honour, especially they who labour in the word and doctrine.... For men shall be lovers of their own selves, covetous,

boasters, proud, blasphemers, *disobedient to parents,* unthankful, *unholy.*

This series of letters to Timothy on the mission field reveals or reinforces the basic principles of authority in the local church and the consequences of rebellion against that authority structure. Going further, Paul again tells what can happen when an unruly child disobeys the divine commandment of honoring his parents: disobedience leading to rebellion, which can progress to being overt, which can progress to hate, and which ultimately can lead to the murder of either or both parents. We read of that daily in the newspapers. Spiritually, I'm sure that open rebellion against parents in one's heart is equivalent to murder, just like lusting in the heart is equivalent to committing adultery.

We need to understand the gravity by which God places ultimate responsibility on parents for the rearing and disciplining of children. The goal is to prevent any seeds of rebellion from entering their hearts from an early age. God knows what the seeds of rebellion can germinate and grow into by the time of the teenage years: hatefulness, disrespect for any and all forms of authority, independence from others, stubbornness, violence, and even murder.

As I have mentioned earlier in this book, God's character never changes. He is the same today as He was yesterday, and He will be the same tomorrow. That is an absolute truth revealed in Scripture. Let us go back several thousand years in time and look at the time when God was first establishing lines of authority and basic rules of government in the Hebrew nation as it progressed through the wilderness areas toward the promised land of Canaan.

Exodus 21:15, 17 established God's attitude toward disobedient, rebellious children. He did not want any child spreading the seeds of rebellion among His new nation. These verses read: "And he that smiteth his father, or his mother, shall be surely put to death.... And he that curseth his father, or his mother, shall surely be put to death." Is any part of that not clear to readers everywhere? God hates rebellion because He witnessed it occurring in Heaven among a third of the angels, and He knows that it ultimately leads to spiritual death for man.

Unfortunately, modern society has been deceived (by very liberal principles of child-rearing) into thinking that it is best for a child's development to allow him to learn independence, speak his mind, go unpunished for bad behavior, and learn his own version of self-discipline from an early age. This freedom of expression will supposedly liberate the child from humanity's hang-ups and allow him to emerge as his "true self" among equals. This kind of rubbish has deceived millions of well-intentioned parents, and the young adults now on our streets and in prison are the fruits of decades of widespread failure to disciple children in the fear (of judgment) and love (in relationship) of God.

Notice that this subject of a man's teaching and discipling his children in submission to God-ordained parental authority is so critical as to be a criterion for screening and approving leadership in the local church. Paul addressed the three main levels of authority in the local church and gave qualifications, the common thread being the requirement that they have ruled their children and households well.

How will you know if this is the case or not? You will know by *the fruit they bear* in the family. Is the wife happy and content? Are the children obedient and submissive to authority? Do the children respect their elders? Are proper care and provisions made for their well-being? If potential candidates for these three positions of authority don't measure up to that standard, Paul said to not appoint them! These three positions of authority are as follows:

- *Bishops*/apostles
- *Deacons*/helps/administrations
- *Elders*/pastors

A person who cannot rule his own house well (and disciple the next generation) is disqualified from having authority in the church because he has not proven himself a good steward of what God has already placed in his hands (wife and children). I have seen the problems in several churches over the years when deacons and elders were appointed because of their popularity, not because of their good spiritual fruit. Their unruly children not only created problems but also influenced other children to be disobedient to their parents. Very few of those unruly children stayed in the Body of Christ when they reached the teenage years or ever had healthy relationships with their parents. They went out into the world.

Look at the company Paul said unruly children keep: the ungodly, sinners, the profane, the covetous, blasphemers, self-loving, and so forth. Disobedient, unruly children become rebellious adults, and there is no place of leadership in the Church of God for them. Rebellion is a spiritual condition of the heart and is always at enmity with God.

7. To Titus: Titus 1:16; 3:1 NLT (emphasis added)

> Such people claim they know God, but they deny him *by the way they live*. They are detestable and *disobedient*, worthless for doing anything good. *Remind the believers to submit to the government and its officers. They should be obedient*, always ready to do what is good.

There are many within the Body of Christ who have not died to self, have not transformed their minds, and have not disciplined their bodies. By their lack of good works or fruit from bad works, their lives deny the influence of Jesus.

Paul here links disobedient believers with detestable people, incapable of producing good works and void of good judgment. He tells Titus to remind the believers that they are to be submitted to the authority of governments in the church *and* in secular government. Titus is also instructed to remind them to do good works. It does not come naturally to the unregenerate human mind, and without Christ even believers who love Christ might not love their fellow man as much as they love themselves.

Let us now finish this subject of submission to authority by looking at the writings of two other prominent writers, Luke and Peter. They learned submission directly from Jesus, and I am sure that it took several years of effort for Peter to finally walk in it, since he was a very headstrong individual who had been used to going his own way.

First is Peter, and our verses are found in 1 Peter 2:13–15; 5:2–6 (emphasis added).

Submit yourselves to every ordinance of man for the Lord's sake: whether it be to the king, as supreme; Or unto governors, as unto them that are sent by him for the punishment of evildoers, and *for the praise of them that do well. For so is the will of God,* that *with well doing* ye may put to silence the ignorance of foolish men.... Feed the flock of God which is among you, *taking the oversight* thereof, not by constraint, but willingly; not for filthy lucre, but of a ready mind; *Neither as being lords over* God's heritage, but being ensamples to the flock. And when the chief Shepherd shall appear, ye shall receive a crown of glory that fadeth not away. Likewise, ye younger, *submit yourselves* unto the elder. (Yea, *all of you be subject one to another),* and be clothed with humility: for God resisteth the proud, and giveth grace to the humble. Humble yourselves therefore under the mighty hand of God, that he may exalt you in due time.

More so in these passages than in others we've looked at are the most difficult principles for most Christians to accept and then live by. What robs many believers of peaceful and contented lives is their rebellion against *secular authority* as manifested in public laws. They may accept spiritual authority but balk at living a lifestyle that consistently obeys all our governmental laws: highway laws, tax laws, marriage laws, firearms laws, employment laws, federal/state/county laws, and so forth.

God placed men and women in positions of authority to write laws for our protection and our good welfare. To rebel against these leaders or their laws is to rebel against God. We are to pray for them: for their salvation, peace, wisdom, vision, knowledge, integrity, and character. Only when the laws of man go against the laws of God do we have a conflict. Then we are expected to pray diligently for God to guide us in what to do, where to go, how to act, and what to say or not say. But—we are not to be defiant toward secular laws.

Notice what Peter said to the various believers scattered among several different countries and cultures in his apostleship: obey them that have rule over you—the kings, governors, and other agents with authority. This admonition is irrespective of which country of origin is on your passport, which form of government you have, which culture you were brought up within, or which religion you claim.

Authorities come to punish evildoers and show appreciation to those who are law-abiding. Peter says that this principle of submission to all authorities is God's will. Our good works in obeying the laws of man put to silence any criticism or disqualification of our testimony by foolish men. We project a positive, godly influence to the world system by our obedience. Our submission to God is not mocked because of our rebellion to the laws of man.

Have you ever witnessed a person of a different faith or religious organization who scoffs at and selectively disobeys some of our nation's laws because his religion doesn't agree with them? How do you and others feel about that person's rebellion? Do you want to be guilty of the same? God wants men everywhere to be obedient and to submit to the laws of the land, regardless of which country or province or state they dwell in.

We are to *be like Jesus:* not lawbreakers, not rebellious in nature, and not turning potential believers against our testimony. The Jewish priests, scribes, and lawyers could find no example of lawbreaking in Jesus' life, whether in the Mosaic Law or the secular Roman law. It wasn't because they didn't look; they worked hard to find something to accuse Him of before the priests and the Romans. Will an examination of our lives show areas in which we are violating laws, statutes, and ordinances?

Ask yourself these few *example questions.* Your answer may reveal that you are not yet fully submitted to the teachings of our Lord Jesus.

1. Do you intentionally drive over the speed limit? (A person with a "fuzz buster" on his dash usually has one in his heart too.)
2. Are all your income streams being reported for tax purposes?
3. Are all your firearms that require legal registration properly registered?
4. Do you ever discriminate at work against any of the federally protected groups of people?
5. Do you adhere to all civil laws concerning real estate transactions, loan applications, and automobile license and registration?
6. Are you diligent in timely and full payment of court-ordered alimony and child support?

These examples of how we may break laws each day show how important it is to get in our place of prayer and die daily to ourselves, to our flesh, and to our rebellious nature.

It is easy to be in rebellion, whether quietly or openly disobedient, in everyday life. Rebellion can manifest itself in many ways, all harmful to relationships and ministry. God equates rebellion to the sin of witchcraft, which was an abomination to Him and which carried the penalty of death under the Mosaic Law. The level of dishonesty or lying or cheating resulting from rebellion can be very low and subtle, but it is insidious and will undermine your credibility. This eventually disqualifies your Christian testimony. When your spheres of influence have been shipwrecked, you cannot be productive for the Kingdom. This is very serious business with God!

Did you please your boss at work with the report he asked for and which you felt was not worth your time? Did you procrastinate and not get it done completely, or did you think up some lame excuse for intentionally disregarding his request? Did you think you could avoid being responsible for the report's not being done if you used the old line "It's easier to get forgiveness afterwards than to get permission beforehand"?

You told your son that you would pitch baseballs with him, but you see that the Braves' game is about to start on television. What do you decide to tell him so you won't miss any of the game on television?

You rented a tiller at the hardware store and agreed to return it by Saturday morning for the next customer reservation. However, you want to make a bigger garden so decide to keep the tiller until Monday and tell them the car broke down and you couldn't get it back in time.

When asked by the home Bible-study group leader to call five families who have been out for a while, you agree to do so, just to sound supportive, but have no intention of making the calls. How do you answer for yourself at the next meeting when asked for a report on those families?

We can live fruitful and victorious lives in Christ when we are sincerely striving to be obedient to all of God's instructions and the instructions of those He sets over us in the church, on our jobs, and at school. The opposite side of this coin is also true; we cannot live fruitful and victorious lives in Christ when we do not sincerely strive to be obedient to all of God's instructions. Often His instructions come to us through His designated authority in our lives, and we need to recognize that fact.

God put authorities and laws in place as a protective framework under which we can live and do good works for His Kingdom and for His glory. Are you going all the way with God or just wading out to the deep part and stopping there? To do the works of Jesus requires total submission and obedience to His Word and His Spirit in all areas of life. *Partial obedience is the same as disobedience.* You cannot walk in lockstep formation with the rest of God's Army if your attitude is one of a renegade, one who walks to the beat of a different drum. Spiritual rebels and renegades are not welcome in the Army of God.

Next is Luke in Acts 20:28. This verse says, "Take heed therefore unto yourselves, and to all the flock, over which *the Holy Ghost hath made you overseers* to feed the church of God, which he hath purchased with his own blood" (emphasis added). Luke tells us that Paul called together the elders of the church at Ephesus and was teaching, advising, testifying, and warning about their spiritual responsibilities in the governing of God's Church. This would be the last time they would see him, and they knew it, so these things were said with great gravity of spirit.

Paul told these ministers in verse 27 that he had not been bashful or timid to declare to them the whole counsel (Word) of God. Paul reminded them that God had appointed them to positions of authority in His Church and that they must also feed the sheep in like manner—*all* of God's counsel, not just the easy parts or well-accepted parts. They were to maintain order and be accountable for the results.

If you had been in the church at Ephesus and one of these elders had spoken correction into your life because he saw your bad fruit on display, would you have listened to him and taken the spiritual medicine needed? If God showed one of the elders that you had hidden sin in your life and that judgment was about to fall on you, would you receive from him that counsel he offered? Perhaps you feel like you've been called to preach, and you think you're ready to start, but one of the elders tells you that your lifestyle and words still require more discipline and testing before trying to speak for God. Could you receive this word and commit it to prayer and positive change while holding in check your desire to go preach right now?

These are but some easy examples of why God establishes levels of authority in the Body. Having authority in God's house is a heavy burden and is not for everyone. You must speak, teach, preach, counsel, administrate, heal, reconcile, and, most importantly, *be an example* in all godliness. You must speak for God regardless of what you feel or what people want to hear.

You need to respect that position of responsibility, whether it comes from the fellow out in the parking lot directing you to the right side when you want to turn left against traffic, or the usher who requests that you stop taking up the entire aisle space by dancing around with abandon while your eyes are closed. If the pastor or one of his ministry staff calls you on the carpet because you mishandled a situation in which someone was hurt, you need to stop being defensive and listen, realizing that he is keeping order in the church and doing what is best for the body. He may ask you to apologize to the hurt party or to make recompense.

Remember, those in authority over the sheep will be held to a much higher level of accountability before God than the individual sheep. We are to respect and to submit to God-ordained authority, or else we are in rebellion. That applies to both the spiritual and the secular powers watching over our lives. The decision is ours to make and will determine how smooth or rough the spiritual course of our lives will be.

Walking in Love

The reason many Christians are ineffective in their attempts to do the works of Jesus is that they lack genuine love for their fellow man. This is often the main reason that the Holy Spirit does not operate the gifts of the Spirit or signs and wonders in a person's ministry. These believers either are devoid of agape love (having lost their first love) or have their love directed at other things besides God and their fellow man. That is hard to say but is very true.

Let's review some things that we know about love and challenge ourselves to perform a self-examination—the condition of our souls, our motives, and the results of our works. The fruits evident to each one of us from this examination will speak loudly about our Christian "love state."

1. God is love. First John 4:7–8, 11–12, 16–18, 20–21 are passages of power that, unfortunately, have usually been relegated to children's Sunday school classes and are not recognized as some of the most profound Scriptures in the New Testament, revealing so much about our Father and our responsibilities to Him and our fellow man in this life.

Beloved, let us love one another: for love is of God; and every one that loveth is born of God, and knoweth God. He that loveth not knoweth not God; for *God is love....* Beloved, if God so loved us, we ought also to love one another. No man hath seen God at any time. *If we love one another,* God dwelleth in us, and *his love is perfected in us....* And we have known and believed the love that God hath to us. *God is love;* and *he that dwelleth in love dwelleth in God, and God in him. Herein is our love made perfect,* that we may have boldness in the day of judgment: because as he is, so are we in this world. There is no fear in love; but *perfect love* casteth out fear; because fear hath torment. He that feareth is *not made perfect in love....* If a man say, I love God, and hateth his brother, he is a liar: for he that loveth not his brother whom he hath seen, how can he love God whom he hath not seen? And *this commandment* have we from him, *That he who loveth God love his brother also.*

Love—that is God in us, not a human emotion in our brains and hormonal glands as we're led to believe by scientific minds. His nature and existence is love itself. When we say we love someone, we are expressing the outward extension of God's Spirit from us (from our spirit-beings, the righteousness of Christ where He dwells) toward another person. When we feel compassion for someone, we are feeling God in us simply wanting to meet that need. He makes us feel the need, and it is up to us to meet it or not.

Forget for the moment our romantic attraction to the opposite sex as being love. I am speaking here of holy God in us; our spiritual connections of love to others are channels of God's Spirit going out from us to reach them. They will feel God emanating from us, and the intensity of their response to God's Spirit will make them feel a certain bond of love. It is that channel of love, which is God in us that we willingly extend outward to others, that is the conduit for good works and the supernatural acts of God to occur. *No love equals no power.*

Note what supernatural principles are described in the above verses, ones that are immutable, absolute in eternity.

- It is of critical importance that humans love one another. This is like saying it is our nature as believers to outwardly display God to all men, at all times, under all circumstances. If we cannot or will not do that, we are not His own. Jesus will not call us His disciples without evidence of sincere, active love (God) shining out from us to others.

- We have to be born of God's Spirit to extend God's love (agape) to others. Some people in darkness are kind, ready to help others, and evidencing what appears to be love for others. However, it is not love (God); it just looks similar to love. Being a good person with the best intentions for others is not love. It is counterfeit love, of the world, the best that unre-generate man can do on his own without God. If God is not the source and the content, it cannot be love.

- When we exhibit or display God (love) to others, He continues to dwell in us, and *our love is perfected* (vv. 11–12.) There are not many things in this life that are perfected, and we are being told of one here. When *He dwells within us* (His Holy Spirit residing in our human spirit) and perfects our love, He then has an ideal, pure channel through which to minister to the outside world. The key is in our willful deci-sion to love our fellow man as we love ourselves: in care, provision, protection, fellowship, and so forth. That requirement and the resulting channel are what opens the supernatural to operate in our lives.

- Our willful love relationship with the outside world maintains our spiritual relationship with God. Do you see how verses 16–17 turn around what was stated in verses 11–12 so that we see the other side of the coin? It is most important that you read these verses and see the distinction. These verses emphasize to us that *we dwell in God* by maintaining a willful love for our fellow man. The other set of verses emphasize that *He dwells within us* because of the outward love shown. Together these show that our outward work of love keeps us in Him *and* Him in us.

- John repeats in verse 17 that this is how our love is perfected. Keep this thought within your mind and meditate upon it: our display of outward agape love to man perfects love (God) in us. The perfection of love in us is our maturity in things of the Spirit. We start approaching the exercise of, operations of, and discipline in the works of Jesus, which amounts to doing the will of the Father. I know that is a lot to digest, but it is meat, not milk, for believers. Do we want to do the will of the Father in our lives? If so, then we need to start doing the works of Jesus! The key is so simple—love your brother as much as you love yourself.

- Love and fear are mutually exclusive in the spirit realm (verse 18). Which do you choose to operate in? When love is perfected by our love for others, fear cannot operate in us. Instead, we operate in love, boldness, faith, and power to achieve good works.

- Verse 21 states that this whole issue of outward love is a *commandment*— it is neither optional nor circumstantial. How many commandments do we read in the New Testament?

2. Faith requires love in order to operate. We looked at that in Scripture in an earlier chapter. You say you operate in faith? Yes, you must exercise faith to appropriate the unseen and bring the unseen into physical reality. But your faith will be weak or unable to operate if you lack love. You cannot pray in faith for my healing if you don't love me as your fellow man. You must have God active in your spiritual life for Him (love) to make you feel my need and have compassion.

   Read the life of Christ and notice the compassion flowing outward from Him to those in need that He ministered to in the crowds. Whether I am a stranger that you've just met or your lifelong Christian buddy, you must have love for me in order to bring healing to my body. This is the same for deliverance ministry, counseling, or any other area of ministry that accomplishes the work supernaturally by God's Spirit. Build up your most holy faith, but *actuate it* through love, and it will produce results (good fruit) in the lives of others. *No love equals ineffective faith.*

3. Jesus said very clearly to His followers and to His personally picked disciples that they (we) must love God with all of their beings and also love their fellow man as they loved themselves. By that unique love (God) in Christians for their fellow man, the world would recognize them as *His disciples*. This is your primary credential for ambassadorship: being His disciple. Man will not recognize your authority or want to hear what you say if you do not come in sincere agape love. *No love equals no disciple.*

4. The outward manifestation of God in you toward others is the light that is supposed to shine into the world. He is that source of light within you. By a choice of your will, you let that light escape into the world of darkness, or not. This quality of being light (and salt) was addressed by our Lord in His teachings. If you hide it under a bushel basket or snuff out the candle, your only source of true light doesn't shine. You are not His disciple, according to Scripture.

The analogy could best be described as though you are an active volcano on the verge of erupting, yet you keep everything capped tightly so the surrounding land does not feel, see, and hear the power bursting forth. God is the Father of Lights; let Him radiate outward from your spirit so His Spirit can affect the world around you so that you can minister effectively to it! *No love equals no illumination of your surroundings, which equals no good works, which equals no good fruit.*

5. One other facet of God's light (love) emanating from believers is the principles of purity and transparency required for effective transmission of light. We are the vessels of God's Spirit, clay containers that hold the indwelling Holy Spirit, the ultimate and desired living tabernacle of His presence on Earth. He dwells in our re-born spirits, the new creatures in Christ Jesus, re-created in purity and holiness and without spot or wrinkle.

   It is the soul (mind, will, and emotions) and body that are unregenerate and in need of perfection so as not to impede the outward transmission of God (love, light) to the world around us. It is the trials, tests, sufferings for Christ, spiritual warfare, and other experiences living for Christ that perfect our salvation and allow the love of God (God Himself) to shine out more brightly through our transformed minds and disciplined flesh, both under submission to and in agreement with our righteous spirits. Only with maturity in the Lord and this perfection process occurring in us are we attaining a state of transparency for maximum transmission of love into the world.

   The Bible gives us a clear example of this with regards to gemstones and precious metals. Most of us would not recognize raw gold ore or silver ore because of its many impurities. We know how dull and rough the naturally occurring gemstones are when found in the ground (like us, when Christ finds us in sin). When cleaned, processed, ground, and polished, however, a gemstone becomes a brilliant stone of high quality. Why does the worth increase dramatically after processing? Answer: because of its new, high level of efficiency in transmitting light! The stone has become much more transparent to light, allowing much more light to escape it, which makes it much more attractive to people and more desirable to obtain.

Extending this further, we are told in Scripture and given examples of how the gemstones and precious metals in Heaven are *totally transparent,* having been purified to perfection. The streets are of pure gold and transparent because there is no longer any hindrance to the transmission of light through the gold. Read some examples of the other gemstones that comprise walls, gates, and columns throughout the city.

Heaven is a city of lights because God is the source of light; He resides there in the center, and no impurities are present to limit His light emanating out in full power from the city through the transparent gems and metals! This is exactly how He wants us to be on Earth. He is within us and wants to shine out in brilliance to the world, only we have imperfections and impurities that prevent or limit Him in most cases.

We are given His charge to *perfect ourselves* so that He is not hindered in giving life-changing, dazzling light (love) to a dying world in darkness around us. Are we allowing His Spirit to purge and purify us in our souls and bodies while maturing us in spiritual things? If not, we will be unable to adequately love our fellow man as we do ourselves and will lead incomplete, unfulfilled lives as believers.

Read 1 Corinthians 13 for a good synopsis of love – recognizing it and understanding its potential to impact our lives and those we meet. It tells us that no matter how high in circles of ministry or operation of the gifts of the Spirit I go, I am nothing without love. Good works done for the poor and the church profit me nothing without love. Love suffers long, is kind, does not envy, does not act impulsively, and is not puffed up with pride. Love does not behave impolitely or unrighteously, is not self-seeking, is not easily provoked, and does not entertain evil thoughts. Love will never rejoice in iniquity but will rejoice in the truth. Love bears all things, believes all things, hopes all things, and endures all things. It never fails. Having love and acting in it is greater (more important, greater fruitbearing) in God's Kingdom than having faith and acting on it.

One other key measuring rod for assessing our degree of active love is found in 1 John 4:20-21.

> If a man say, I love God, and hateth his brother, he is a liar: for he that loveth not his brother whom he hath seen, how can he love God whom he hath not seen? And this commandment have we from him, That he who loveth God love his brother also.

I want to give an example of how some people are blind to their lack of love for their fellow man and how that condition prevents them from doing the works of Jesus and robs them of the fulfillment and rewards that come from producing abundant good fruit. Some years ago, we were attending a church in a new place of residence when God began to deal with both Lee and me about not being fed as sheep in the flock of God. This was odd since I was teaching the young adults' class and Lee was working with Children's Church, both doing the kinds of things that needed responsible believers.

As that awareness of and desire for God grew in us during the year that we were there in that church, I began to observe things that we had previously taken for granted and accepted as normal. We rarely saw any visitors, there was rarely any ministry to people at the end of the service, and there was no life in the sermons from the pulpit. Messages from the pulpit seemed too canned, like they had been prepared by someone else or pulled out of some sermon binder and merely warmed over to serve again. Church members were the same group (no growth), all sitting in the same pews each service, and there were no signs of any expectations of change.

This began to bother me, since God was challenging us about not being fed. One weekend the pastor asked me if I would like to go with him to visit several church members. He said he regularly did that and would like for me to come along with him. He did not know that God had been making my wife and me restless about our lack of shepherding and not being fed spiritual food in the church. (Those kinds of things are between you and God, to be committed to prayer and fasting and not to be blabbed about foolishly to others.)

I observed as the pastor was asked to pray for people; they had pains, had been feeling bad, had loved ones unsaved, and many other things. Since God had sensitized me about these issues recently, I listened closely to his prayers while we were there in the homes of members. I realized what I had never taken notice of before—the pastor prayed *for God to heal* their sickness and diseases, he prayed *for God to send* someone to bring the good news (gospel message) to their loved ones, and he prayed *for God to deliver* family members from addictions.

Never was there any acknowledgment by the pastor of his responsibility or interest in doing these works. His prayers were not directed to the root source of the disease or addiction, taking authority over them in Jesus' name. The prayers were passive, as though he expected that if he lifted them up to God, then He would somehow provide the active healing or deliverance ministry. I kept looking for some signs of action on the pastor's part: spiritual battle, taking authority, using the name of Jesus with authority, use of anointing oil, or other tools of warfare.

None were there—only a sympathetic prayer voicing understanding of the situation followed by the reassurance "We'll be praying for you" when we left. As we were riding back to the church, I was thinking about these issues and wondering why God had raised my awareness of these topics, since I was not in the ministry. I was not prepared for what happened next, which made clear to me some of the reasons for the current status quo at the church and the lack of fruit in this person's ministry.

As we rode along, we approached a man walking on the side of the road facing toward us, heading in the opposite direction from us. When the man came into clear view, the pastor stopped talking, slowed the car, and focused on the man. I assumed that he knew the man and might stop. But the man walking toward us was unshaven, looked a bit ragged, and had that blank look in his eyes that indicated a hard life and possibly some addiction problem. As we got close to the man, the pastor leaned over by my shoulder as close as he could get to the window so he could shout at the man, "Get off the road, you dirty bum!"

His face was flaming red and his eyeballs bulging when he screamed those words at the man alongside the road. I was in shock at those emotional words. Then with the man not seeming to have heard the spleen vented, the pastor straightened himself up and continued to tell me that those old drunken bums should clean themselves up and get into church; they had no business out walking around looking like that, in that condition.

I asked him if he knew the man, and he said that no, he didn't. Right then, I knew why there was no power in that ministry—there was no love for his fellow man, no compassion, and no practical understanding of what the ministry of Jesus is about. Shortly thereafter, my wife and I left that church.

No love equals no ministry. No ministry equals no good works or good fruit. No love equals no power to change. We are to go into the highways and hedges, compelling them to come in to the House of God. We are to lay hands on the sick and oppressed, exercising the authority and power given to us by Jesus, *expecting* them to be healed.

When we look around in church, our spirits ought to leap within us at the sight of alcoholics, prostitutes, pimps, murderers, addicts, former prisoners, wealthy scoundrels, renegades, and such that have been brought into the church by the members to receive the message of hope, of power, and of redemption through the blood of Jesus. Regardless of how grisly they look or how bad they smell, we need to get them exposed to the love of Jesus, and then the other issues will take care of themselves.

If they are not in the church, then we need to reach them right out in their world: the street corners, alleys, jails, clinics, and along the streets and highways. I'm afraid that we are not getting the job done. Instead, many believers would look down their snooty noses at that group in church because they wouldn't be dressed appropriately, might not smell like they've bathed and perfumed that morning, or would not conduct themselves with the "dignity" expected in God's house. These types of believers are perhaps worse off than the sinners who are there to find God.

Summary

Let us now put into a perspective of spiritual service the issues that have been discussed. We are not His disciples if we do not *love* Him and our fellow man. We are of little value to the Kingdom of God if we do not *serve* Him and serve our fellow man. We are given authority and power to *do the works* of Jesus, which are directed toward our fellow man. We will be judged by our Lord for the fruit we bear that gives glory to God. Jesus is the Head of the Church; He has given us Himself as the Word of Truth and Life; He has sent us His Holy Spirit to guide, comfort, and empower; and He has delegated to all believers the use of His name and His authority for effective ministry to the world of darkness.

Each one of us has to ask ourselves the question, Do I hunger and thirst for the things of God? If we don't, we need to search our hearts and see where the problem(s) lies. Otherwise, we will be people who keep the pews warm and never live in the privileges of God as His children and will never receive the eternal rewards for service. For those believers who do hunger to please God by doing what He has called them to do and who want all that He makes available to them, He has much in store for them.

How do we present ourselves as believers to the world? How do all of these principles of discipleship and ministry come together in practical application for each of us? Here is a suggested list for us to place under a refrigerator magnet and look at each day. These concepts should challenge us to extend ourselves further than we've ever imagined in serving our God and our fellow man. They will make us better fishers of men, and we will one day hear these words of our Master that will provide ultimate fulfillment to our lives: "Enter in to the joys of Paradise, My good and faithful servant."

1. We are to love one another openly for the world to see.
2. We are to pray for one another.
3. We are to disciple new believers.
4. We are not to judge one another.
5. We are to submit ourselves unto one another and unto authorities over us, becoming properly fitted together in the body.
6. We are to strengthen, encourage, and edify one another.
7. We are to serve one another.
8. We are to plant ourselves in the local church in order to provide the use of our parts of the body (finger, toe, arm, pancreas, and so forth).
9. We are to forgive one another.
10. We are to be displaying all manner of fruits of the Spirit-led life to one another: gentleness, kindness, humility, faithfulness, patience, joy, peace, self-discipline, sincerity, politeness, and others.
11. We are to be doing the works of Jesus in the world.
12. We are to bear good fruit from our works.
13. We are to tithe faithfully to the local church and to give generously to support other ministries bearing good fruit.

May God's richest blessing be upon your head as you strive to be that man or woman in Christ that He has created, called, and chosen you to be.

CPSIA information can be obtained at www.ICGtesting.com
Printed in the USA
LVOW062154020312

271300LV00002B/1/P